**Editor**
Lorin Klistoff, M.A.

**Editor in Chief**
Karen J. Goldfluss, M.S. Ed.

**Cover Artist**
Marilyn Goldberg

**Illustrator**
Teacher Created Resources

**Art Manager**
Kevin Barnes

**Imaging**
Craig Gunnell

**Publisher**

*Mary D. Smith, M.S. Ed.*

**U.S. HISTORY**

# READERS' THEATER

### Bringing the past to life!

- Original scripts based on historic events and highlights
- Introductory background information to set the stage for each script
- Reader's response and extension activities
- Convenient, reproducible pull-out scripts for each student

Teacher Created Resources

**Author**

*Robert W. Smith*

**Teacher Created Resources, Inc.**
6421 Industry Way
Westminster, CA 92683
www.teachercreated.com
ISBN: 978-1-4206-3997-1

© 2008 Teacher Created Resources, Inc.
Made in U.S.A.

Teacher Created Resources

# TABLE OF CONTENTS

## What Is Readers' Theater?

Readers' theater is drama without the need for costumes, props, stage, or memorization. It is performed in the classroom by groups of students who become the cast of the dramatic reading. The players employ their oral reading skills, creative expression, and dramatic voice to communicate the mood and the meaning of the script.

Students should have practiced the script several times over a few days and be well versed in the meaning of the text and well practiced in using correct pronunciation, proper voice inflection, appropriate changes in volume, and various nuances of expression to create an effective dramatic reading.

## Why Use Readers' Theater in Social Studies?

Children need to live history. A steady diet of textbook readings and vague focus questions tend to make history a series of meaningless, disconnected events. The vibrant story of our nation's life becomes dry, tasteless, and boring. Students need to have a sense of involvement with the human dramas that make up the history of men and women down through the ages.

Children can relate to the tension of a young married couple escaping from slavery to freedom. They can imagine the terror of wading through the water at Omaha Beach as bullets strike their buddies. They can visualize Hugh Glass crawling across rocks and cactus on his 100-mile journey to safety. Using readers' theater and other dramatic activities is a creative way to grab student imagination and focus it on a period of history.

## Literature Connections

The stories that unfold in these readers' theater scripts can be the spark that spurs student interest in some of the best children's historical literature. Books such as *Bud, Not Buddy* and *Out of the Dust* provide special insights into the nature of the Great Depression. *Ashes of Roses* and *Lyddie* make factory life personal and real to young readers. Each unit in this book highlights an effective and engaging piece of children's literature to help you extend the lesson.

# INTRODUCTION (cont.)

## Writing Dramatic History

Children become more involved in historical events when they immerse themselves in the action. Having children create scripts based on the historical epochs they are studying is a good way of creating students who think about historical events and consider the consequences of individual human actions and cultural interactions. Encourage your students to use the dramatic format and the suggestions in each extension activity to create their own readers' theater scripts.

Use the discussion activities on the last page of each unit to help students internalize the motives of the characters in the scripts or to draw closure after the script has been performed.

## Targeting the Topics

You will want to use the scripts in this book as you teach individual units of American history. There are representative scripts for virtually every age from the Colonial and Revolutionary periods through the American Civil War and the Westward Movement of the American People to the Great Depression and World War II and the man on the moon.

## Working with the Scripts

Each script is designed to illuminate one facet of the historical sweep of a given era or one significant event. The background information preceding each script gives a brief historical context to help your students place the event in terms of time and place. Depending upon circumstances, you may want to do several scripts simultaneously with your class as you finish a semester of work or do the scripts along the way as you finish individual topics in American history. Teachers whose time for teaching history in the upper elementary grades is limited may choose to use these scripts and the background information as the primary vehicle for social studies instruction and reinforce these tools with selected textbook readings or high quality historical fiction in children's literature. (**Note to Teacher:** It is important to review the content of each script prior to classroom study. Choose scripts that are appropriate to your curriculum and are suitable for your students.)

## Selecting Teams and Leaders

If all of your class will be doing readers' theater dramatic readings, select good readers and good leaders for each script. These leaders will often do the narration or provide a strong voice for one of the longer or more important dramatic parts. They should help resolve some questions of pronunciation and the meanings for words that are unfamiliar to some of the students. You will also need to assist teams with these tasks and resolve occasional disputes related to meaning or role selection.

## Selecting Teams and Leaders *(cont.)*

Assign each of the student script leaders a team composed of students with varying reading abilities. You may want shy children, struggling readers, or students just learning English to have more limited roles in their first readers' theater experiences. However, all students should have ample time to practice with their fellow team members so that the performance is effective and interesting to the student audience.

## Staging

Your classroom is the stage. Place the proper number (four to seven) of stools, chairs, or desks to sit on in a semicircle at the front of your class or in a separate staging area. You may use simple costumes, but generally no costume is expected or used in this type of dramatization. If you have plain robes or simple coats of the same color or style so that everyone looks about the same, this can have a nice effect. Students dressed in the same school uniform or colors create an atmosphere of seriousness. Props are not needed, but they may be used for additional effects.

## Scripting

Each member of your group should have a clearly marked, usable script, as well as the complete unit with background information, extensions, and discussion questions. Students should be able to personalize the script with notes indicating when they speak, which part or parts they are reading, and mechanical notes about pronunciation of specific words and phrases or sentences they intend to emphasize in some dramatic way.

## Performing

Students should enter the classroom quietly and seriously. They should sit silently and unmoving on the stools or chairs. Performers should wait with heads lowered, or they should focus on an object above the audience. When the narrator starts the reading, the actors can then focus on their scripts. The actors should look at whoever is reading, except when they are performing.

## Movement, Memorization, and Mime

Experienced readers' theater actors may add gestures or other movements to their lines. Some actors may choose to introduce mime to a performance if it seems to fit. Several actors will learn their lines so well that they have virtually memorized them. Some students will want to add props or costumes, as the circumstances allow. More involved actors often begin to add accents to a character in the script.

## Assessment

Base performance assessments on the pacing, volume, expression, and focus of the participants. Student-authored scripts should demonstrate general writing skills, dramatic tension, and a good plot. Class discussions should reflect serious thought, use of the background information, and references to the text of the script.

# READERS' THEATER

# THE STARVING TIME

# BACKGROUND: THE STARVING TIME

## The Founding of Jamestown

The first permanent English settlement in North America was founded at Jamestown, Virginia, by English settlers in 1607. More than half of the men were gentlemen adventurers who were untrained for any useful work. They expected to find fortunes in gold and gems as the Spanish had in Mexico and South America. In its first few years of existence, eight thousand of the first ten thousand settlers at Jamestown died. Starvation and disease killed most of them, but Native American attacks and accidents also took their toll.

The colony would probably have failed completely had it not been led by Captain John Smith, a shrewd and stubborn leader. He required every person who wanted to eat to work, including those gentlemen who weren't used to hard labor. He kept an uneasy peace with the local natives and also mapped much of the area. However, Smith was injured and had to return to England. His successor was unable to force the adventurers to work and the entire colony gradually fell victim to a terrible winter of death.

**Captain John Smith**

## A Winter of Despair

"The Starving Time" is set during the bitter cold winter of 1609–1610. Of the 500 settlers who lived in Jamestown in the fall of 1609, fewer than 60 survived the winter. So many people died that some weren't even buried until spring. Many settlers perished from famine (not having enough food to eat), from exposure to extreme cold, and from diseases. Some died in sporadic attacks by Native Americans who were angry that the settlers were stealing their food and treating them unfairly. Some settlers had attacked Native Americans out of fear, frustration, and greed.

Some of the houses were destroyed by settlers looking for wood to burn for fires. A few of the settlers were farmers and craftsmen with useful skills for the building of a colony, but many were men who simply had no skills and no desire to do any useful work. They were not cooperative in a society that absolutely needed everyone to work together in order to survive. Women and children were the first victims of starvation and illness, but most of the men died as well. Diseases included malaria, typhoid fever, dysentery, and other illnesses that sapped the settlers' strength and made them more vulnerable to the effects of extreme cold and inadequate food.

The members of the colony were in such bad shape that they boarded a ship and started back to England entirely abandoning the colony. They met British ships a few miles away carrying new settlers and fresh supplies. The settlement at Jamestown and the colony of Virginia eventually succeeded, but it had been a very close call.

# SCRIPT SUMMARY: THE STARVING TIME

"The Starving Time" is a fictional account of a meeting in the settlement of Jamestown, Virginia, at the end of the terrible winter of 1609–1610 when the colony is on the brink of total collapse. Almost all of the women and children and most of the men have died of starvation, extreme cold, several terrible illnesses, and attacks from the once-friendly Native Americans who inhabit this area.

The narrator sets the scene for the readers. There are four men who attend the meeting. Sir Thomas Gates is the new governor who recently arrived from England after being shipwrecked near Bermuda. Captain George Percy was the acting governor of Jamestown through the terrible winter. Reverend Waite is a clergyman. John Laydon is a carpenter, a practical man who recognizes that the people of Jamestown and the leadership are largely responsible for their own troubles.

The script explains through the discussion of these men how waste and laziness led to their critical shortage of food. The delusions of the gentlemen adventurers who spent their time searching for nonexistent gold and gems has left the colony without enough working men to make the colony survive. In the end, the colony is abandoned and the people are sailing away when help from England arrives.

## Assignment

Read the readers' theater script entitled "The Starving Time." Work with your group to prepare for the performance. Share your interpretation of the script with your team members. Suggest ways to effectively communicate the story's message. Practice the script several times until you and your fellow actors are effective communicators. Present the readers' theater script to the classroom.

## Extensions: Writing and Literature

- Rewrite the script from the point of view of Native Americans observing the settlement at Jamestown, the gentlemen adventurers, or of a woman or child living in the settlement. Present your script to the class.

- Write a readers' theater script based on an event in the Colonial period of American life. Use one of the suggested ideas listed below or your own choice.

    A slave makes the Middle Passage across the Atlantic.

    A woman is tried at the Salem witch trials.

    The first Thanksgiving is held in Plymouth.

- Read the novel *The Serpent Never Sleeps* by Scott O'Dell about Pocahontas and the settlement at Jamestown or read *The Double Life of Pocahontas* by Jean Fritz. Create a script based on one event from the story. Present your script as a readers' theater.

# SCRIPT: THE STARVING TIME

The following script is a fictional account of a meeting at the end of the terrible winter of 1609–1610 when the settlement of Jamestown came close to total failure. There are five parts.

**Narrator:** The time is May, 1610, in Jamestown, Virginia, after a terrible winter which fewer than 60 settlers out of 500 have survived. The settlement had been on the edge of survival since it was founded in the spring of 1607. Most of the settlers were spoiled gentlemen adventurers who were not prepared by personality or training for a life of extreme physical labor and privation. Only a few hard-working farmers, some servants, and an occasional craftsman were scattered among the gentlemen. Sir Thomas Gates, the new governor, has just arrived in the settlement that is in ruins. He joins three men who are sitting in the ruins of a house. Captain George Percy is the acting governor. Reverend Waite and John Laydon, a carpenter, are the other two.

**Sir Thomas Gates:** We've just arrived from England. Our ship was wrecked in a hurricane near Bermuda, and we had to spend several months there building two small vessels to get us here. This is not the settlement I expected. We heard that Jamestown was becoming prosperous. What has happened?

**Reverend Waite:** This has been a winter of terror and terrible sadness. I feel at times that we have been abandoned by God. We spend most of our time burying our dead. We're almost too weak to do a decent Christian job of it. We barely get them beneath the earth and say a few prayers.

**John Laydon:** At least they're mostly buried. Some have not been so fortunate. We're grateful to see you, Governor, but we have nothing to offer you. I hope you brought food. Our people are starving to death.

**Captain Percy:**    We've had a terrible time. The winter has been bitterly cold. So many men have been ill that many of the houses and parts of the fortification have been used for firewood. This has been especially troublesome because the savages have determined to destroy us. We can't go outside the settlement without being attacked by a swarm of arrows fired from a dozen different hiding places.

**John Laydon:**    Jamestown was a terrible land for a settlement in the first place. It's not easy to defend and the chief of the local Indian tribe has determined to destroy us. When Captain Smith was here, we often were able to trade with the Indians for corn and other food, but no longer.

**Sir Thomas Gates:**    Where are all the gold and riches we were told about?

**Reverend Waite:**    The gold is in the fool heads of the investors in England and our own gentlemen. They spent the entire summer last year digging up fool's gold and looking for gems and riches. It was the only work those worthless gentlemen did.

**John Laydon:**    It was different when John Smith was governor. He made the rule, "If you do not work, you do not eat," and he enforced this rule.

**Captain Percy:**    I took over when Captain Smith was wounded and left for England in October. We thought there was plenty of food in the settlement and easy hunting in the forests, but the Indians killed many of our hunters. The corn was quickly devoured, some of it by rats. Wild pigs and hens are in the forest, but we cannot get to them.

**Reverend Waite:**    We've had terrible sicknesses, too. This land is swampy. The drinking water is bad and often not fit for drinking. We've had typhoid fever, dysentery, and all other manner of illness. Most of the women and children here have died.

**John Laydon:** We have eaten everything we could. You will notice there are no dogs or cats. They have long since been in the cook pots. We have eaten every form of snake and creature that has been unlucky enough to be seen. The few pigs and hens that were in the settlement were eaten by the gentlemen. They were not inclined to share, either.

**Reverend Waite:** Many of us have eaten our boots and shoes, as you can plainly see. Our people are nearly as barefoot as the Indians!

**Captain Percy:** We don't even know what happened to some of our residents. Desperate for food, they went outside the fort and never returned— either killed or captured by the natives. I don't know which would be worse. What shall we do?

**Sir Thomas Gates:** I do not see any choice but to return to England. We can load your survivors on our two boats and hope we make it back to England.

**Narrator:** That is exactly what was done. On June 7, 1610, the settlers climbed aboard ship and set off for England. They sailed only a short distance before they encountered a fleet of ships carrying 300 more settlers and a new governor. They returned to Jamestown, and this time, they stuck it out.

# READER'S RESPONSE: THE STARVING TIME

## Directions

- These discussion activities and questions may be used in small groups or with the entire class. They may also be used by the actors as a part of their preparation for the reading.
- Refer to the script "The Starving Time" when responding to all questions. You may also find useful facts in the background information section.
- Make notes on the lines provided below each question before your group discussion.

## General Discussion

1. What was the most serious problem facing the settlers in Jamestown? Defend your response with references to the script.

   _____
   _____
   _____

2. What mistakes did the leaders and members of the colony at Jamestown make which placed them in so much danger of death and failure?

   _____
   _____
   _____

3. If you had been a leader of the colony at Jamestown, what would you have done to save the colony or your own life?

   _____
   _____
   _____

4. Why do you think the colonists did not get along with the Indians who were native to the area? In your opinion, who was to blame for the conflicts between settlers and natives?

   _____
   _____
   _____

5. With whom do you sympathize most among the suffering colonists at Jamestown? Explain your choice.

   _____
   _____
   _____

## Making It Personal

What role would you have liked to live at Jamestown—gentleman adventurer, reverend, captain, carpenter, farmer, Native American, mother, child, or servant? Why?

_____
_____
_____

# READERS' THEATER

# THE DECLARATION OF INDEPENDENCE

# BACKGROUND: THE DECLARATION OF INDEPENDENCE

## Conflict with England

In the early 1770s, the American colonies became increasingly frustrated and angered by British efforts to impose several new taxes and increase their authority over the colonial governments with tough, new laws. Many Americans believed that it was time to make a complete break from Great Britain and create a new nation. The Second Continental Congress met in May 1775 with the colonies in a state of crisis.

The tea parties in Boston and elsewhere had demonstrated colonial unity and infuriated the British. The battles at Lexington and Concord had stiffened British resolve to teach the colonists a lesson. Armed men gathered into companies called militias in all of the colonies to prepare for the coming conflict. In June of 1775, the Congress appointed George Washington Commander-in-Chief of the Continental Army. In June 1776, a resolution for independence was presented to the Congress.

## Writing the Declaration

On June 11, 1776, five members of Congress were appointed to draft a declaration of independence that could then be voted on by the full Congress. The members were John Adams, Roger Sherman, Benjamin Franklin, Robert Livingston, and Thomas Jefferson. The committee chose Thomas Jefferson, a popular supporter of independence and a gifted writer, to create the original draft. Jefferson spent a little over two weeks writing his draft of the declaration. He showed his final version to the other committee members who made a few suggestions and changes.

## The Signing

The document was submitted to Congress on June 28, 1776. On July 2 the Congress discussed Jefferson's draft. The discussion lasted for two days. Congress made about eighty changes in the text, sometimes changes of words or punctuation, and sometimes they took out entire paragraphs. For example, Jefferson, himself a slaveholder, wanted to declare an end to slavery—but Southern representatives would not accept this.

In the late afternoon of July 4, the delegates were satisfied with the Declaration and it was adopted. In August, John Hancock signed the document as President of the Continental Congress and that made it legal. He wrote his name very large, he claimed, so that King George could read it without his spectacles. Fifty-five members of Congress signed the document pledging their lives, their fortunes, and their sacred honor to secure their liberty. The Declaration of Independence was printed and proclaimed throughout the colonies. General Washington had it read to his soldiers.

## The Language of the Declaration: Words, Terms, and Expressions

*endowed*—given by birth to all people

*unalienable*—cannot be taken away (today "inalienable" is used)

*consent of the governed*—the people accept the rule of law

*light and transient causes*—frivolous or silly reasons

*hath shewn*—has shown

*usurpations*—taking power by force

*absolute Despotism*—absolute rule by a tyrant (King George)

*candid world*—honest observers

*assent*—approval

*legislatures*—places where free men make laws

*a right inestimable to them*—a right beyond any price

*formidable*—needed or used (in this usage)

*dissolved Representative Houses*—ordered legislatures closed

*manly firmness*—courage

*tenure*—length of time

*eat out their substance*—cost money (taxes) needed by the people

*standing armies*—soldiers stationed near or in a town

*quartering troops*—stationing troops in homes and villages

*trial by jury*—the right to a fair trial

*plundered*—destroyed and looted

*ravaged*—destroyed and ruined

*domestic insurrections*—riots

*British brethren*—British citizens

*consanguinity*—having the same ancestry and heritage

*Supreme Judge of the World*—God

*rectitude*—strict honesty and moral character

*absolved from all allegiance*—no longer connected by citizenship

*levy war*—declare war

*contract alliances*—make treaties with other nations

*establish commerce*—start businesses

*Divine Providence*—God

# SCRIPT SUMMARY: THE DECLARATION OF INDEPENDENCE

This script, "The Declaration of Independence," is an abbreviated version of the original Declaration. Some repetitious portions have been removed, but the essential thrust of the document has been retained. The opening preamble explains to the new country, to Britain, and to all nations and times (a candid world) the justification for independence. The remainder of the document details the many violations of personal and colonial liberties endured by the colonists. All of the blame for these injustices and complaints is assigned to King George III.

The American colonists perceive themselves as British citizens who have been deprived of their rights by a dictatorial, capricious, overbearing, and abusive king. The list of injuries to colonial self-rule include taxation without representation by the British Parliament, the presence of a standing army in the colonies (and in peoples' homes) during peacetime, and a failure to respect laws passed by the colonial assemblies.

The final section of the Declaration declares the freedom of the American colonies from British rule, their desire to be an independent nation, and their belief that God is on their side as they pledge everything they own and life itself for freedom.

## Assignment

Practice the readers' theater script for the Declaration of Independence. Work with your team to prepare for the performance. Carefully study the language of the Declaration on page 15 to become familiar with the meanings of unfamiliar words and phrases. The four readers should stress the reasonable and careful nature of the decision in the first part, the preamble, to the document. They will want to read the list of complaints with a sense of anger and sadness. The final declaration of freedom should be full voiced, powerful, and defiant.

## Extensions

- Practice reading the script with some low background music. Use an instrumental version of one or several patriotic songs. These might include "The Star Spangled Banner," "God Bless America," or "The Battle Hymn of the Republic." Present your dramatic reading at Open House, Grandparents' Day, History Day, Memorial Day, or another school event.

- Use the Internet or books to find a copy of the *Declaration of Sentiments* written by Elizabeth Cady Stanton and modeled on the Declaration of Independence. This document became an important milestone in the history of women's efforts to secure equal rights. Prepare a dramatic reading of this document.

**Reader 1:** A Declaration by the Representatives of the United States of America, in General Congress assembled.

**Reader 2:** When in the Course of human Events, it becomes necessary for one people to dissolve the political bands which have connected them with another, and to assume among the Powers of the earth, the separate and equal station to which the Laws of Nature and of Nature's God entitle them, a decent respect for the opinions of mankind requires that they should declare the causes which impel them to the Separation.

**Reader 3:** We hold these truths to be self-evident, that all men are created equal, that they are endowed by their Creator with certain unalienable Rights, that among these are Life, Liberty, and the pursuit of Happiness. That to secure these rights, Governments are instituted among Men, deriving their just powers from the consent of the governed,—

**Reader 4:** That whenever any Form of Government becomes destructive of these ends, it is the Right of the People to alter or abolish it, and to institute new Government, laying its foundation on such principles and organizing its power in such form, as to them shall seem most likely to effect their Safety and Happiness.

**Reader 1:** Prudence, indeed, will dictate that Governments long established should not be changed for light and transient causes; and accordingly all experience hath shown, that mankind are more disposed to suffer, while evils are sufferable, than to right themselves by abolishing the forms to which they are accustomed.

**Reader 3:** But when a long train of abuses and usurpations, pursuing invariably the same Object evinces a design to reduce them under absolute Despotism, it is their right, it is their duty, to throw off such Government, and to provide new Guards for their future security.

**Reader 2:** Such has been the patient sufferance of these Colonies; and such is now the necessity which constrains them to alter their former Systems of Government.

**Reader 4:** The History of the present King of Great Britain is a history of repeated injuries and usurpations, all having in direct object the establishment of an absolute Tyranny over these States.

**Reader 1:** To prove this, let Facts be submitted to a candid world.

**Reader 2:** He has refused his Assent to Laws, the most wholesome and necessary for the public good.

**Reader 3:** He has forbidden his Governors to pass Laws of immediate and pressing importance, unless suspended in their operation till his Assent should be obtained; and when so suspended, he has utterly neglected to attend to them.

**Reader 4:** He has refused to pass other Laws for the accommodation of large districts of people, unless those people would relinquish the right of Representation in the Legislature, a right inestimable to them and formidable to tyrants only . . .

**Reader 3:** He has dissolved Representative Houses repeatedly, for opposing with manly firmness his invasions on the rights of the people . . .

**Reader 1:** He has made Judges dependent on his Will alone, for the tenure of their offices, and the amount and payment of their salaries.

**Reader 2:** He has erected a multitude of New Offices, and sent hither swarms of Officers to harass our People, and eat out their substance.

**Reader 3:** He has kept among us, in times of peace, Standing Armies without the Consent of our legislatures . . .

**Reader 4:** For quartering large bodies of armed troops among us . . .

**Reader 1:** For cutting off our Trade with all parts of the world . . .

**Reader 3:** For imposing Taxes on us without our Consent . . .

**Reader 2:**     For depriving us, in many cases, of the benefits of Trial by Jury . . .

**Reader 3:**     For suspending our own Legislature, and declaring themselves invested with Power to legislate for us in all cases whatsoever . . .

**Reader 1:**     He has plundered our seas, ravaged our Coasts, burnt our towns, and destroyed the lives of our people . . .

**Reader 4:**     He has excited domestic insurrections amongst us, and has endeavored to bring on the inhabitants of our frontiers, the merciless Indian Savages, whose known Rule of Warfare is an undistinguished Destruction of all Ages, Sexes and Conditions . . .

**Reader 2:**     Nor have we been wanting in attentions to our British brethren . . . They too have been deaf to the Voice of Justice and Consanguinity. We must, therefore . . . hold them as we hold the rest of mankind, Enemies in War, in Peace Friends.

**Reader 4:**     We, therefore, the Representatives of the United States of America, in General Congress, Assembled, appealing to the Supreme Judge of the world for the Rectitude of our Intentions, do, in the Name, and by the Authority of the good People of these Colonies, solemnly publish and Declare,

**Reader 3:**     That these United Colonies are, and of Right ought to be, Free and Independent States; that they are Absolved from all Allegiance to the British Crown, and that all political connection between them and the State of Great Britain, is and ought to be totally dissolved;

**Reader 2:**     And that as Free and Independent States, they have full Power to levy War, conclude Peace, contract Alliances, establish Commerce, and do all other Acts and Things which Independent States may of right do.

**Reader 1:**     And for the support of this Declaration, with a firm reliance on the Protection of Divine Providence, we mutually pledge to each other our Lives, our Fortunes, and our sacred Honor.

# READER'S RESPONSE: THE DECLARATION OF INDEPENDENCE

## Directions

- These discussion activities and questions may be used in small groups or with the entire class. They may also be used by the actors as a part of their preparation for the reading.
- Refer to the script "The Declaration of Independence" when responding to all questions. You may also find useful facts in the background information section.
- Make notes on the lines provided below each question before your group discussion.

## General Discussion

1. What was the most serious grievance or complaint against the government of Great Britain listed in the Declaration of Independence? Explain your choice.

_____

_____

_____

2. What truths does the Declaration say are self-evident?

_____

_____

3. Do you think the men who signed the Declaration completely believed in these truths? Explain your answer.

_____

_____

_____

4. Do you think all Americans, most Americans, or some Americans believe in these truths today? Explain your answer.

_____

_____

_____

5. The right to make and enforce laws is of major importance in a free country. How do Americans make laws today and do the people have enough influence on the making of laws in the United States today? Explain your response.

_____

_____

_____

## Making It Personal

The men who signed the Declaration of Independence pledged their lives, fortunes, and sacred honor to achieve independence. They would have lost everything if they failed. Would you do the same today against a foreign power who controlled your country? What would you have to lose?

_____

_____

_____

# READERS' THEATER

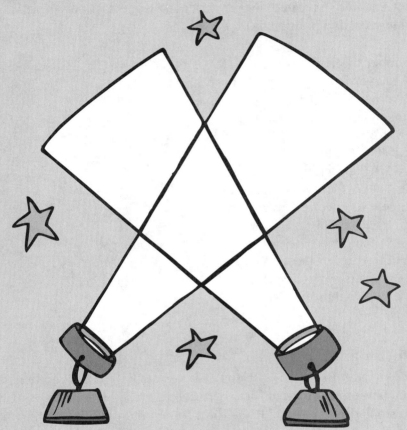

# MR. PRESIDENT

# BACKGROUND: MR. PRESIDENT

## The Men Who Wrote the Constitution

The fifty-five men who met together in Philadelphia to write a constitution for the new nation were a remarkable collection of talented, educated, and experienced leaders. These practical men were often successful merchants, lawyers, and politicians.

The most important member of the convention was a 36 year-old scholarly lawyer from Virginia, James Madison, who became known as the "Father of the Constitution." Madison believed the country needed a new form of a strong, national government with supremacy over the states. He believed such a government would reduce economic and social differences between the states. George Washington wanted the new government to have real power. He knew from his Revolutionary War experiences, the dangers that would exist if the government remained a weak and squabbling collection of independent states. Other advocates of a strong government were Alexander Hamilton, Benjamin Franklin, and Edmund Randolph.

## A Clash of Ideas

There were many sources of arguments and serious disputes during the convention. These included the role of slavery in the new nation and the conflicts between large and small states. The large states were worried they would be crippled by laws and taxes forced upon them by the small states. The small states feared they would be outvoted and overwhelmed by the more populated larger states like Virginia.

## The Idea of the Presidency

The entire idea of the presidency was a new and dangerous concept to many of the founders. Some, like Elbridge Gerry and John Dickinson, feared the idea of an elected king, a ruler with too much power who would destroy their liberties and ignore the wishes of individuals and states. They distrusted power and wanted a very weak executive leader. They didn't even want him to have a fancy title that sounded royal.

On the other hand, Alexander Hamilton, a young New York representative and a rising political figure, supported a very strong leader with near king-like powers. Madison and Edmund Randolph favored a very strong presidency with a great deal of power. They feared the nation would be destroyed by foreign powers or remain a group of squabbling small states if they didn't have a strong president.

Despite their differences, the founders hammered out a compromise that has worked remarkably well for over 200 years. The arguments about how strong a president should be are still debated today.

# SCRIPT SUMMARY: MR. PRESIDENT

This script is an abbreviated account of the intense discussions about the idea of the presidency conducted by the delegates to the Constitutional Convention. The narrator introduces the discussion and sets the lines between those who favor a strong chief executive, a powerful president, and those who want the role of the president tightly limited.

James Madison and Alexander Hamilton took the lead in forcefully arguing for a strong, powerful, almost king-like president. Elbridge Gerry and John Dickinson were leading members of the convention who wanted the president to be quite weak and totally controlled by laws and Congress. They even argued about the name for the president with Madison and Hamilton favoring a fancy, almost royal title, and Dickinson and Gerry wanting no suggestions of power or royalty.

Benjamin Franklin, in his usual shrewd way, gets to the gist of the problem and suggests a solution that allows enough power but not too much. His suggestion for the simple term "Mr. President" is respectful but doesn't have any suggestion of royal power or hints of special privilege. The title, "Mr. President," is still used today.

## Assignment

Read the readers' theater script entitled "Mr. President" about the Constitutional Convention. Work within your group to prepare for the performance. The seven readers need to create a sense of the intensity of the argument and the reasons for it. Share your interpretation of the script with your team. Practice different expressions that would help highlight the serious passages and the humor in certain situations. Make sure each reader is well-practiced, clear, loud, and easy to understand. Present the script to your audience.

## Extensions: Writing and Literature

- Choose a related topic to create your own readers' theater script. Write a script based on one of the events listed below related to the writing of the Constitution or another one of your choice related to the Constitutional Convention. Use *Shh! We're Writing the Constitution* by Jean Fritz and other books as sources of ideas.

    The Virginia Plan is introduced to the Convention.

    The New Jersey Plan is debated.

    The final signing day at the Convention

    Patrick Henry "smells a rat" and refuses to attend the Convention.

    A hot day in the State House as members quarrel and the temperature rises

    The debate over slavery

- Practice and present your script to the class.

# SCRIPT: MR. PRESIDENT

This script is an abbreviated account of the discussions at the Constitutional Convention relating to the nature of the Presidency that the Founding Fathers were creating. There are seven speaking parts.

**Narrator:** The delegates to the Constitutional Convention were deeply divided over who should lead the new government they were creating. Some delegates, like Alexander Hamilton, wanted a president to serve for many years or even a lifetime, like a king. Others wanted the office to have little real power and the term to be only one or two years.

**Edmund Randolph:** What we need to create, Gentlemen, is a strong national government with a congress to make laws, a president to enforce those laws, and a judicial branch to determine that they are fair and equitable. Our poor nation right now is a collection of weak and arguing states that do not trust each other. They impose taxes on each other, and sometimes are even at the point of war.

**John Dickinson:** We just got rid of one king. I'll not have another one. Keep the states as they are.

**Elbridge Gerry:** We were sent here to revise the Articles of Confederation—not to form a nation with a king or some other powerful leader.

**Alexander Hamilton:** This country needs strong leadership—otherwise it is going to be gobbled up by European empires. What we need is a president for life.

**John Dickinson:** No, I don't agree. A president with very little power is what we desire. The weaker he is the safer we will be. One year is long enough for any president.

**James Madison:** He has to be strong or this nation will blow away like leaves in the wind with every state going broke, being swallowed up by other countries, or always getting into wars.

**Elbridge Gerry:** I don't trust any ruler. All he will want to do is raise taxes and get us into war. He will end up a king with a different title.

24

**James Madison:**  This country needs leadership. We cannot afford to have a weak or feeble chief executive. He must be able to act with force when necessary.

**Narrator:**  Many delegates were fearful that the presidency would pass from father to son like a monarchy or that the president would rule the country without regard to the congress or the rule of law.

**Elbridge Gerry:**  Why does it have to be a president for life—why not six years or four or one year?

**Alexander Hamilton:**  Well, it would be embarrassing to have a lot of ex-presidents wandering around like ghosts with nothing much to do.

**Benjamin Franklin:**  But suppose you had a lifetime president or even one with a six-year term, and he turned out to be a worthless president. What could you do about it? We might have to arrange some way to get rid of a president who is incompetent or sick or who commits a crime. Otherwise, we might have to shoot him.

**Narrator:**  Many of the delegates were amused by Ben Franklin's suggestion, but they also recognized the problem. What would ex-presidents do? Would they go back home to their businesses and farms or would they find other jobs in government? The delegates were also uncertain what to call the leader of this new office they were creating.

**Elbridge Gerry:**  How will we address this president?

**Alexander Hamilton:**  I think that he should be called His Highness or His Excellency.

**Elbridge Gerry:**  Sounds just like a king to me or some other high-fallutin' gentry.

**Benjamin Franklin:**  How about just plain, Mister, such as Mr. Randolph or Mr. Madison?

**Elbridge Gerry:**  How about Mr. President? It's simple, dignified, and it doesn't put on airs.

**John Dickinson:**  That sounds just right.

# READER'S RESPONSE: MR. PRESIDENT

## Directions

- These discussion activities and questions may be used in small groups or with the entire class. They may also be used by the actors as a part of their preparation for the reading.
- Refer to the script "Mr. President" when responding to all questions. You may also find useful facts in the background information section.
- Make notes on the lines provided below each question before your group discussion.

## General Discussion

1. With which character in the script do you most agree? Why?

   _____
   _____
   _____

2. Do you think presidents should have more power or less power than they have today? Prepare at least three reasons to support your opinion.

   _____
   _____
   _____

3. What are the qualifications, abilities, and skills you want a president of the United States to possess? Explain the value of each qualification you suggest.

   _____
   _____
   _____

4. How often should presidents be elected? Give two reasons supporting your choice.

   _____
   _____
   _____

5. What should be done about a president who commits a crime, gets extremely ill, becomes mentally incompetent, or is extremely incompetent?

   _____
   _____
   _____

## Making It Personal

Would you want to be President of the United States when you grow up? Write at least three serious, thoughtful, and intelligent reasons for your answer.

   _____
   _____
   _____
   _____

# READERS' THEATER

# HOMECOMING

# BACKGROUND: HOMECOMING

## The Louisiana Purchase

The Louisiana Territory was purchased by representatives of President Jefferson from the French emperor, Napoleon Bonaparte. It extended from the Mississippi River to the Rocky Mountains and from the Gulf of Mexico to the Canadian border. It was an area of roughly 830,000 square miles.

In 1803, Jefferson chose his private secretary, Meriwether Lewis, as the captain of an expedition to the newly purchased land to explore what they had bought. He had Lewis trained in botany, celestial navigation, practical medicine, and natural history. Lewis chose William Clark as his coleader because he thought that an expedition of this magnitude needed two leaders. They complemented each other, and their personal friendship was so strong that they never had a serious disagreement on the three-year-long trip.

A few months into their journey, Lewis and Clark met Sacagawea and her French fur-trapper husband, Touissant Charbonneau, at Fort Mandan. They hired Charbonneau as a guide, but they knew they especially needed Sacagawea, a Shoshone Indian, to help guide them and to convince the Shoshone to trade them horses for the journey over the Rocky Mountains. Sacagawea had been captured by Hidatsa Indians when she was twelve. She lived with the Hidatsa until she was sold to Charbonneau as his wife.

As they traveled west, Lewis and a few men finally met the Shoshones. The Indians thought these white men might be enemies or a trick arranged by their Blackfeet enemies. Sacagawea's arrival with the main group convinced them otherwise, and she was joyfully reunited with her brother, Cameahwait, who was now chief of the tribe. Cameahwait reluctantly agreed to trade horses to the expedition for some of the trading goods that Lewis had brought along. Lewis and Clark hired a Shoshone they named "Old Toby" to guide them through the Mountains.

Eventually, the expedition found the Columbia River and made small boats to carry them down the river to the Pacific Ocean. The expedition spent the winter in what is now Astoria, Oregon, and started home in the spring of 1806. They arrived in St. Louis on September 23, 1806. The journey took two years, four months, and nine days. Most Americans had given them up for dead. Along the way, they discovered 178 new kinds of plants, 122 new species of animals, and more than 40 Indian tribes. Their expedition also helped establish the United States' claim to the Oregon territory they passed through.

# SCRIPT SUMMARY: HOMECOMING

The narrator introduces the audience to the situation facing the members of the Lewis and Clark expedition. They have reached the headwaters of the Missouri River, and they know they are near Shoshone territory. The company is desperate to trade for horses with the Shoshone. They need them to get across the Rocky Mountains.

Captain Lewis and George Drouillard meet some local Indian women whom they believe to be Shoshone and ask directions to a Shoshone village. The women lead the men to their village, but they are not welcomed or believed by the Shoshone chief, Cameahwait. He distrusts their motives and is not impressed by their references to the president. Lewis stresses the gifts the expedition has brought for the Shoshone and the size of the expedition that is coming. The chief is not impressed. He thinks they may be working for enemies, such as the Blackfeet.

The arrival of the main group of the expedition changes his mind when he meets Sacagawea, his long lost sister who was captured by another tribe when she was a child. Chief Cameahwait is delighted to see his sister again and changes his attitude toward the expedition.

## Assignment

Read the readers' theater script "Homecoming." Prepare for the performances and share your interpretations of the scripts with the class.

## Extensions: Writing and Literature

- Write a script based on one of the events listed below or another one related to the Lewis and Clark expedition.

    Jefferson and Lewis plan the expedition.

    Life at Fort Mandan with the Indians

    Hard times crossing the mountains

    Lewis and Clark report back to President Jefferson.

    Lewis gets shot by one of his own men.

    Sacagawea rescues the journals from the river.

    Sacagawea carries her baby across the country and back.

    Events on the expedition told from the viewpoint of York, Clark's slave, who was a vital member of the expedition

    Events on the expedition from the point of view of Sacagawea

- Read *Streams to the River, River to the Sea: A Novel of Sacagawea* by Scott O'Dell. Use one episode or a chapter as the basis for a readers' theater script about Sacagawea's experiences on the expedition.

# SCRIPT: HOMECOMING

This script is an abbreviated account of the meeting between the expedition and the Shoshone people. (Much of the actual communication was done in sign language, the universal language of the Plains Native Americans, and with translations from English to French to Hidatsa to Shoshone and back.) The script requires five speakers.

**Narrator:** The members of the Louis and Clark Expedition have reached the headwaters of the Missouri River where it divides into three rivers. Following the Jefferson fork, the captains are desperate to find the Shoshone Indians in order to get horses and to find a route over the Rocky Mountains. They are now sure that no river exists to carry them over the mountains, and they have to have horses for travel over the mountains. Captain Lewis and two men have gone on ahead to find the Shoshones and scout the trail.

**Captain Lewis:** George, we have to find the Shoshones soon. If it gets any closer to winter, we'll never make it over those mountains.

**George Drouillard:** The Shoshone woman said that we are close. She was captured from her village near the three forks of the Missouri, which we just passed a few days ago. She remembered that mountain that looks like a beaver's head. We've got to be going in the right direction.

**Captain Lewis:** There's a Native American up ahead. He must be Shoshone. Let's catch up with him.

**Narrator:** The men race after the Shoshone, but he vanishes. Soon they come upon three Shoshone women gathering roots for food.

**Captain Lewis:** Please listen to me. We have come a long way to meet the Shoshone people. Please take these gifts and lead us to your village where we may talk with your chiefs.

**Narrator:** The two girls and the older woman are terrified by the appearance of these explorers, but they are gratified by the gifts. They agree to lead them to their camp. As Lewis approaches the camp with his men and the three women, he puts his rifle away as a sign of his peaceful intentions and takes out an American flag that he carries. A huge crowd of Shoshone suddenly surround them and escort them to the village where the three women display their gifts. The leader, Chief Cameahwait, approaches them. He is not too friendly or trusting.

**Cameahwait:** Who are you? Why have you come to our village?

**Captain Lewis:** I represent the President of the United States in Washington. We are on a great journey to the far ocean beyond the mountains.

**Cameahwait:** I do not know or care of this president. Why do you come to our village? Who sent you?

**Captain Lewis:** We have come to bring gifts to your people and to trade for horses that we need to go over the mountains. We also need to find the pass through these mountains.

**Cameahwait:** I think that you come as an enemy. I have heard of white people, but I have never seen one. We have no horses to trade. I do not trust you. We should kill you now.

# SCRIPT: HOMECOMING (cont.)

**Captain Lewis:**   I come with many people. They are carrying many gifts and many goods for trade. We travel with a Shoshone woman, who has a child. We come in peace. A war party does not travel with a woman or child. She has shown us the way to her homeland so that she can see her people again. She was captured four years ago by the Hidatsa Indians.

**Cameahwait:**   Maybe the Blackfeet or the Hidatsa have sent you as a trick.

**Captain Lewis:**   We have nothing to hide. We travel with many things you have never seen before. Besides the Shoshone woman, we have a black man who wears buffalo hair. He is a giant among men. We have many guns and much ammunition and a gun which kills in silence.

**Cameahwait:**   Where are these marvels? I think you are sent by the Blackfeet.

**Narrator:**   A Shoshone scout reports that he has seen a great group of men, including one black man and an Indian woman carrying a child. As the group enters the camp, Sacagawea comes forward. Suddenly, she points to her mouth to indicate she is one of them. She looks very carefully at Cameahwait and then covers him with her robe or blanket to indicate they are related.

**Sacagawea:**   My brother, Cameahwait! My brother, do you not remember your sister? Do you recognize the little sister who used to tease you all the time? Do you remember your sister?

**Cameahwait:**   My sister, you have returned from the dead. Come, we must have a great feast to celebrate your return. Bring your friends into our village. Let me see the wonders you have brought.

# READER'S RESPONSE: HOMECOMING

## Directions

- These discussion activities and questions may be used in small groups or with the entire class. They may also be used by the actors as a part of their preparation for the reading.
- Refer to the script "Homecoming" when responding to all questions. You may also find useful facts in the background section.
- Make notes on the lines provided below each question before your group discussion.

## General Discussion

1. Why is the story called "Homecoming"?

_____

_____

_____

2. Do you think the Shoshone tribe had good reason to distrust the motives and intentions of the whites? Explain your answer.

_____

_____

_____

3. What would probably have happened if the expedition had not been able to trade for horses?

_____

_____

_____

## Making It Personal

How would you feel if you were to meet a long-lost brother or sister? Would you feel joyful or sad? Why?

_____

_____

_____

_____

Would you like to have been on the Lewis and Clark expedition? Why?

_____

_____

_____

_____

Which member of the Lewis and Clark expedition would you most like to meet and become friends with? Why? What would you talk about?

_____

_____

_____

_____

# READERS' THEATER

# MOSES LEADS HER PEOPLE

# BACKGROUND: MOSES LEADS HER PEOPLE

## Who's Who on the Underground Railroad

The people who worked on the Underground Railroad often used real railroad terms to distinguish their roles in bringing slaves to freedom. *Pilots* were courageous men and women who went to the South to encourage slaves to run away from their owners. Many of these were former slaves, but some were whites. Regardless of color, these pilots were subjected to jail, torture, or hanging if they were caught.

*Conductors* of the Underground Railroad didn't take tickets. They guided slaves from one hiding place to another. The conductor might even hide the fugitive slaves in plain sight as personal servants or slaves, bury them under a wagonload of hay, or move the slaves at night to secret locations. The *stationmaster* of the Underground Railroad was an individual or family who provided a hiding place, such as barns, attics, wells, or caves for fugitive slaves. The *passengers* were the runaway slaves.

## Harriet Tubman

The greatest conductor (and sometime pilot) of the Underground Railroad was a runaway slave known to history as Harriet Tubman and to the people she helped escape as Moses. Born one of eleven children in a slave family, she was often mistreated and beaten by her master. He often rented her out to other owners. She was once hit on the head so hard by an overseer that she suffered a kind of drowsiness the rest of her life if she was not active. Finding that she was going to be sold to another owner, Harriet decided to escape alone because her husband and brothers were reluctant to join her.

Harriet ran away from her owner in Maryland and got to Pennsylvania, a free state. She tried to return and rescue her husband, but he had already remarried and refused to flee. Gradually, Harriet established a route of Underground Railroad stations and made about 20 trips into southern states, rescuing her two brothers, many other members of her family, and over 300 other slaves. Rewards for her capture posted by slave owners totaled over $40,000. During the Civil War, Harriet served as a spy, scout, and nurse for the Union army. She set up her own home as a refuge for freed slaves in need after the war.

# SCRIPT SUMMARY: MOSES LEADS HER PEOPLE

"Moses Leads Her People" describes one of Harriet Tubman's daring efforts to free her family and friends from slavery. The narrator introduces the episode with a brief history of Harriet Tubman's own escape from slave territory in Maryland to the free state of Pennsylvania. William Still is a dedicated leader of the Underground Railroad who is reluctant to support Harriet's desire to go to the South and become a "conductor" leading other slaves to freedom. Harriet overcomes his resistance and goes back to Maryland armed only with her courage and a pistol, determined to rescue her sister and her sister's children from the slave pens where they are being sold.

Harriet sneaks her family out of the auctioneer's holding pen and starts north with her family and other slaves who want to be free. They travel by night and hide during the day along a route where other members of the Underground Railroad provide food and a place to hide. Harriet refuses to allow any slave to quit and return to his or her master because it would put all of the fugitives in danger. Eventually, they reach the safety of Philadelphia, and Harriet is on her way to becoming the Moses of her people. She would make about 20 trips into slave states to bring more than 300 slaves to free soil.

## Assignment

Read the script about Harriet Tubman's dramatic rescue of her family. Work within your group to prepare for the performance. Share your interpretations of the script.

## Extensions: Writing and Literature

- Write and perform your own readers' theater script based on one of the events below or another one related to the Underground Railroad.

   Thomas Garrett loses everything he owns in support of runaway slaves.

   Henry "Box" Brown mails himself to freedom.

   Levi Coffin welcomes a fugitive slave family.

   Anthony Burns is recaptured and returned to slavery.

- Read *Taking Liberty: The Story of Oney Judge, George Washington's Runaway Slave* by Ann Rinaldi. Choose a chapter, episode, or event in the story to use as the basis for a readers' theater script. Write and produce the script for your class.

# SCRIPT: MOSES LEADS HER PEOPLE

This script is an account of one of Harriet Tubman's trips to the South to free other slaves. There are six speaking parts.

**Narrator:** In 1849 Harriet Tubman learned that she was about to be sold, so she decided to escape while she was still in Maryland, next to the free state of Pennsylvania. She left her husband, who was unwilling to go with her, and traveled by foot mostly at night. She made contact with stationmasters of the Underground Railroad who guided her to Philadelphia. There she met William Still, a leading member of the antislavery society, who helped her get settled.

**Harriet:** I have a job and my freedom, Mr. Still, but it isn't enough. My brothers and sister, parents, and friends are still human property. There are more than three million of my people in slavery. I must go down to the South, like Moses, to bring my people to freedom.

**William Still:** I understand your dedication, Harriet, but all of our conductors are men. Going to the South is terribly dangerous. You are a fugitive. Once you cross the line, you are a slave again. The slave catchers and patrollers are brutal men. They get paid for you whether you are dead or alive.

**Harriet:** Nobody cared I wasn't a man when they tied me to a mule or put an ax in my hands. I have a pistol. I don't intend to get caught, and I won't be taken alive. I have saved a few dollars, and as soon as I have enough, I plan to go back for my family. Can you find out anything about them through your contacts in Maryland?

**Narrator:** William Still discovered that Harriet's sister, Mary Ann, was to be sold at an auction. Harriet traveled back to Maryland, going from one Underground Railroad station to another. She arrived in Cambridge, Maryland, armed with her pistol and a great deal of courage. She met Mary Ann's husband, John Bowley, a free black, in a barn.

**John Bowley:** Harriet, I am so happy to see you, but they already have Mary and our three children in the slave pens. The auctioneer is going to sell them this afternoon.

**Harriet:** Wait until the auctioneer goes to lunch. Write a note saying that these four slaves were bought by a wealthy planter and that you are to take them to him. The guards will not expect a forgery. Slaves aren't supposed to read or write. Bring them to the old farmhouse at the edge of town. They're friends. Hide there until night.

**Narrator:** Bowley did as Harriet directed and that night, Mary Ann, her husband, and three children got into a small fishing boat in the Bay of Baltimore and sailed to the city of Baltimore where Harriet met them. They slipped out of the city in the night with three more fugitive slaves from the shipyards.

**Mary Ann:** The sky's overcast. How are we going to find the Drinking Gourd to point us north? We could get lost.

**Harriet:** No, our father taught us that the moss grows on the north side of the tree. We can feel the trees.

**Narrator:** By the time they had traveled a few miles on foot, Mary Ann's youngest child was fussy, and one of the fugitive slaves with them was beginning to complain.

# SCRIPT: MOSES LEADS HER PEOPLE *(cont.)*

**Harriet:** Mary Ann, give this medicine to Annie. We can't afford to have her crying. Sound carries a long way in the woods.

**Mary Ann:** Do we have to? Will it hurt her?

**Harriet:** It's a sleeping potion. She'll be fine. We can't take chances.

**Slave:** Are you sure you know where we're going? If we go back now, they may never know we left. I don't want to get caught. I'm heading back.

**Narrator:** Harriet draws her pistol from her a bag and points it at the men.

**Harriet:** Nobody leaves. Nobody quits. You endanger us all if you do. Believe me, I'll shoot anyone who runs. We're bound for freedom, and there's no turning back.

**Narrator:** They arrived at a dirt cellar near the edge of a field of potatoes.

**Harriet:** We stay at this potato cellar tonight. No talking. It's going to be very crowded. There's barely room for us to fit, but it won't be the worst. Tomorrow we travel in a wagon under a load of hay. We will be hiding in attics and barns and in a tunnel near a ditch. It's a long way, but we will make it.

**Narrator:** They traveled for a week from one station to another along a network of farms, Quaker meeting houses, and abandoned sheds until they reached the safety of Philadelphia and William Still's home. Mary and her family were sent north to Canada, and Harriet headed back south after a few months to rescue more of her family. Harriet Tubman made 20 trips into slave states to bring members of her family, friends, and other slaves to freedom. She became known as "Moses" to the people she helped. She was so feared by slave owners that they offered a $40,000 bounty for her—dead or alive.

# READER'S RESPONSE: MOSES LEADS HER PEOPLE

## Directions

- These discussion activities and questions may be used in small groups or with the entire class. They may also be used by the actors as a part of their preparation for the reading.
- Refer to the script "Moses Leads Her People" when responding to all questions. You may also find useful facts in the background section.
- Make notes on the lines provided below each question before your group discussion.

## General Discussion

1. What character traits and personal attitudes helped Harriet lead fugitive slaves to freedom?

_____

_____

_____

2. What were some of the things and personal relationships that a slave had to give up if he or she became a fugitive?

_____

_____

_____

3. What problems would challenge an escaped slave once he or she was in a free state?

_____

_____

_____

4. Describe some of the places a fugitive slave would hide in during his or her run to freedom?

_____

_____

_____

5. Why do you think white antislavery individuals, such as the Quakers and abolitionists, were opposed to slavery in the South?

_____

_____

_____

## Making It Personal

Imagine that you are an African-American slave in the South during the time of Harriet Tubman. Would you have taken the chance and run to freedom knowing that you faced death, torture, mutilation, or whipping? Explain your choice.

_____

_____

_____

# READERS' THEATER

# STEALING FREEDOM

# BACKGROUND: STEALING FREEDOM

## The Escape of William and Ellen Craft

William and Ellen Craft made one of the most daring escapes in the dark history of slavery. They traveled from Macon, Georgia, in the Deep South to Philadelphia, Pennsylvania, on their own. William and Ellen had been slaves all of their lives. Ellen was a very light-skinned black. She met William Craft in Macon. Rather than have their children born into slavery, the couple decided to escape, even though they knew that fugitives in the Deep South were usually caught, whipped, and often tortured to death.

They had saved some money from tips and small gifts they received as servants. Ellen disguised herself as a white man, cut her hair into a masculine style, wore a man's suit, and covered her face with a bandage to hide her features and indicate a serious toothache. She wrapped a sling over her right arm so that she couldn't be forced to write her name because as a slave she was never allowed to learn how to read or write. Ellen could speak with a white accent. They traveled as William Johnson and slave. Both William and Ellen had obtained passes from their owners to visit relatives for a week at Christmas.

## Nearly Caught

They started off by train and were nearly caught immediately by William's master who had become suspicious. Then Ellen rode in the railroad car right next to a white man she had known for years who tried to carry on a conversation. Later on a steamboat to Charlestown, South Carolina, Ellen was berated by a white army officer for spoiling her slave because she let him eat scraps off her plate.

The couple traveled north by steamboat and on several trains. Several officials tried to prevent them from traveling north. Ellen's persistence and cool courage forced each of these officials to back down. William and Ellen eventually made it to Philadelphia where they received help from the abolitionist, William Still. When their former owners heard about the Crafts' successful escape, they sent agents to locate them and have them arrested. Believers in the antislavery cause hid the Crafts for a time. Finally, the couple went to England where they stayed until the end of the Civil War.

# SCRIPT SUMMARY: STEALING FREEDOM

"Stealing Freedom" describes one of the most spectacular and romantic slave escapes in the history of African-Americans striving to find freedom. William and Ellen Craft were slaves living in Macon, Georgia, a city in the Deep South, a long way from the free states of Pennsylvania and Ohio. Because they wanted their children to be born into freedom, they decided on a very clever but dangerous plan of escape. Ellen, a light-skinned Negro, disguised herself as a white man with a facial bandage covering a terrible toothache. Her husband traveled along as her loyal slave.

They traveled north on trains and steamboats, often encountering problems with officials who did not think William's "white owner" should treat his slave so compassionately. Several officials were determined to prevent them from going into free northern states for fear that William would run away from his owner. Ellen had to muster a great deal of courage and play the part of a rich Southern gentleman to convince these people to let them reach Philadelphia.

Even when they reached freedom in the North, their owners had them followed, and the couple eventually had to move to England until the Civil War was over. The story of their courage, resourcefulness, and love is a very powerful tribute to the desire of all people to live in freedom.

## Assignment

Read the readers' theater script "Stealing Freedom" about the dramatic escape of William and Ellen Craft. Share your interpretations of the scripts with the group. Students may be able to do accents for this script.

## Extensions: Writing and Literature

- Write and perform your own readers' theater script based on one of the events listed below or another one related to the Underground Railroad.

    Eliza Harris runs across the frozen Ohio River with her child in her arms.

    Margaret Garner chooses death over slavery.

    Henry "Box" Brown mails himself to freedom.

    Lear Green hides in a trunk and is shipped to freedom.

- Read *Trouble Don't Last* by Shelley Pearsall about a young boy's run to freedom. Choose one chapter, episode, or event to be the basis for a readers' theater script. Write your script and produce it for the class.

# SCRIPT: STEALING FREEDOM

This script is an account of the escape of William and Ellen Craft from Macon, Georgia, to Philadelphia, Pennsylvania. There are seven speaking parts. Some speakers can perform two roles.

**Narrator:** William and Ellen Craft lived in Macon, Georgia, in the Deep South. They had been slaves all of their lives. Ellen was a very light-skinned black slave. She was given as a wedding gift to the owner's white daughter who lived in Macon, Georgia. Ellen grew up as a household servant and became a skilled seamstress. Sometimes she earned small tips for her work. When Ellen was 18, she met her future husband who worked in a cabinet shop. Although he was a slave, his owner allowed William to keep a little of his pay. He also earned small tips from other odd jobs. William and Ellen decided to marry.

**Ellen:** William, I love you deeply, but we must get out of this land before we have children. I don't want my children born as slaves and owned by my master. I won't have it.

**William:** My first owner sold my parents to different planters. I never saw them again nor did they see each other ever again. My brothers and sisters were each sold to different slave buyers as I was growing up. Right now I have a better owner than most slaves do, but he could sell me tomorrow. I could be led away in chains to work hundreds of miles away, and I'd be forever separated from you. Our only hope is freedom, and I think I have a plan that will work.

**Ellen:** We have to escape, but Macon, Georgia, is hundreds of miles from any Northern state. We could be caught by bounty hunters or slave catchers before we reach the Ohio River and the free states north of it. We don't know the way, and we would be alone against the world with no one to help us. We'd never survive alone in the mountains, swamps, or wild regions like some slaves have done.

**William:** Runaways hardly ever make it from as far south as we live. They are usually caught, whipped, attacked by dogs, branded, sold farther south to cotton farmers, or tortured to death.

**Ellen:** What is your plan, William?

**William:** Take me north on the train as your slave.

**Ellen:** What are you talking about?

**William:** I've been thinking this out very carefully for some time. I'm dark-skinned and nothing will disguise my looks. But you are very light-skinned and could almost pass for being white.

**Ellen:** Maybe in the dark, but I'd quickly be discovered. White men would notice the difference. I don't look that much like a white woman, and even a white woman traveling with a slave would have trouble going where she wanted when we got close to the northern states.

**William:** True, but a white man with his slave would hardly be noticed. You'd have to cut your beautiful hair into a white man's style and wear some men's clothes. Your face is too soft and womanly so we'd have to hide it somehow.

**Ellen:** A toothache! Old man Carothers has had a bandage over his face for a month. It would hide most of my face. I can't read or write though, and travelers have to sign their names on ship manifests and other documents. We aren't even allowed to learn how to even write our own names, but I can talk like a white. I used to imitate all of the white people when I was growing up.

**William:** You could have a broken arm or a serious disease and carry your right arm in a sling. Then you couldn't be expected to write. It would also give you an excuse to need your slave with you.

**Ellen:** This may work. But when we start, William, I'm not turning back. I'd rather die like a dog than be brought back. We go together—all the way to freedom or death!

**William:** All the way to freedom or death. We will steal ourselves and our freedom. The best time to leave is at Christmas. White folks are distracted at that time of the year.

| | |
|---|---|
| **Narrator:** | Ellen made a man's suit and both slaves got Christmas passes from their owners allowing them to stay with family for a few days. They traveled as William Johnson and his slave. By the time they were missed, they hoped to be safe in the North. They boarded the train just before Christmas and walked into danger almost immediately. As a slave, William had to ride in the baggage car. While sitting in a corner of the car, he saw his master checking every railroad car searching for him. His master had become suspicious and was checking to make sure he hadn't run away on the train. Ellen, in the meantime, had problems of her own. A white man she had known for years sat down next to her in the passenger compartment. |
| **Train Passenger:** | Where are you traveling, sir, at this time of year? You don't look well. |
| **Ellen:** | (*her voice muffled by the bandage*) I'm traveling to Virginia to meet relatives. I've never been there. I have a terrible toothache. I've had it for weeks. I fell and cut my arm and hit my jaw. I haven't felt right since. |
| **Train Passenger:** | I know a good doctor at our next stop. Perhaps you should stop and see him. |
| **Ellen:** | I think not. I'll see my family's doctor in Virginia when I get there. I'm going to just rest now. |
| **Train Passenger:** | Suit yourself. |
| **Narrator:** | They left the train and boarded a steamboat bound for Charlestown, South Carolina. Ellen let William eat scraps off her plate. He was feeding her because her arm was supposed to be badly injured. William was required to sleep on the deck without food or water as there was no other place for slaves. |
| **Army Officer:** | You're spoiling that slave, you know. You treat him like a favored child or pet. These blacks need to be kept in their place. |
| **Ellen:** | I'm not feeling well. My arm is hurt, and he feeds me. |

**Army Officer:** That's all well and good. But you're letting that slave eat the scraps off your own plate. That's disgusting! He'll forget his place. Slaves need to be whipped good and often. I'd be glad to give him a good thrashing right now if you'd like. It would teach him a lesson.

**Ellen:** I can handle my own business and my own slaves without any interference from you, thank you.

**Army Officer:** You're making a mistake. Take my word for it. Next thing you know, he'll be running away to the North. Tell you what. I'll give you a $1,000 for that slave right now. I could use one of his size to handle the horses, and you won't have to worry about him escaping. I'll teach him some . . .

**Ellen:** No, he's been in my family a long time. He's trusted, and I need him.

**Army Officer:** Pity. You're making a big mistake.

**Ellen:** I don't think so.

**Narrator:** In Charleston, Ellen was challenged by a tough port official who disliked the idea of letting slaves travel north. Ellen lets her anger work for her.

**Port Official:** Sir, you can't take that slave on the steamboat, and you don't want to. You're heading into free states and that slave is likely to just up and run away.

**Ellen:** William has been with my family a long time. I need him.

**Port Official:** I can't let you take him. There are too many runaway slaves in the North, and you haven't signed the manifest.

**Ellen:** I can't sign. My arm is broken. I paid for our passage, and I'm boarding the ship. I am a Southern gentleman. I have urgent business in Washington, and I will not have my business interfered with. Now get us on that ship!

**Port Official:** All right, sir. I'll let you board, but mind my words. That slave will be up North and free in a week.

**Narrator:** They sailed by steamboat to Wilmington, North Carolina, and then rode trains to Richmond and Fredericksburg, Virginia. They boarded a steamboat to Washington, DC, and rode a train to Baltimore, Maryland, where they switched trains for the trip to Philadelphia. Here they were stopped by a determined railroad agent.

**Railroad Agent:** Mister, you can't take that slave with you to Philadelphia. It's a hiding place for fugitive slaves. He'll run away as soon as he sets foot in the city, or some abolitionist will turn his head with radical ideas. He can't go.

**Ellen:** I am ill, and I need William's help. He has always been very loyal.

**Railroad Agent:** You can't trust any slave. They'll all run at the first chance. I'll not allow him to travel on the train.

**Ellen:** I come from one of the best families in Georgia. I paid for my ticket. William will ride in the baggage car as usual. We are going on this train, or I'll contact higher authorities!

**Railroad Agent:** Okay, but you've been warned. You better keep a chain on that fellow, or he'll be free in no time.

**Narrator:** She got away with it. William and Ellen arrived in Philadelphia where they contacted William Still, a famous stationmaster of the Underground Railroad. He hid them for a few weeks and then sent them on to Boston, but their masters found out where they were and had them followed. Two years after William and Ellen started their journey, they sailed to England, where they remained until the end of the Civil War.

# READER'S RESPONSE: STEALING FREEDOM

## Directions
- These discussion activities and questions may be used in small groups or with the entire class. They may also be used by the actors as a part of their preparation for the reading.
- Refer to the script "Stealing Freedom" when responding to all questions. You may also find useful facts in the background section.
- Make notes on the lines provided below each question before your group discussion.

## General Discussion
1. What were the personal dangers faced by William and Ellen Craft if they were caught before they reached the free state of Pennsylvania?

   _____

   _____

   _____

2. Who do you think had the harder time during the escape—William or Ellen? Explain your choice.

   _____

   _____

   _____

3. Which person posed the most serious obstacle to the success of the escape of William and Ellen Craft? Explain your choice.

   _____

   _____

   _____

4. What attitudes held by white slave owners may have helped William and Ellen before and during their journey?

   _____

   _____

   _____

5. What kind of life did William and Ellen face if they stayed in Macon?

   _____

   _____

   _____

## Making It Personal
Put yourself in the place of William or Ellen Craft. Describe your fears and feelings before the escape attempt and during the journey to freedom.

   _____

   _____

   _____

# READERS' THEATER

# THE DEFENSE OF LITTLE ROUND TOP

# BACKGROUND: THE DEFENSE OF LITTLE ROUND TOP

## Civil War Battles

The American Civil War was fought in 10,000 different places. There were skirmishes between a few dozen men in unmarked fields, at river crossings, in cornfields, or behind stone fences. It was fought in gigantic pitched battles between huge armies of men hurling themselves into bullets, bayonets, and cannons, often fired at point-blank range. Some of these great battles were at Bull Run, Vicksburg, Atlanta, Petersburg, and Gettysburg.

## Gettysburg

In 1863, Robert E. Lee decided to invade the North hoping to bring the war to a victorious end for the South by exploiting the war-weariness of the North. On July 1, 1863, Confederate and Union forces clashed by accident at Gettysburg, a small town in rural Pennsylvania. In three days of brutal warfare, Lee tried to destroy the Northern armies and convince the North to accept the division of the Union. Fighting with fewer men, less supplies, and unable to secure a tactical advantage on the ground, Lee's army was halted and defeated by Union forces, but it was a very close fight during the first two days. The final effort on July 3, an attack by Confederate General George Pickett's division, failed and his division was virtually annihilated by Union troops. Lee was forced to retreat back to Virginia having suffered over 28,000 casualties. Union dead and wounded were over 23,000.

## Little Round Top

The crucial battle-within-a-battle at Gettysburg was fought on a hill called Little Round Top at the extreme end of the Union army. This hill was held by a regiment of soldiers from Maine commanded by Colonel Joshua Lawrence Chamberlain, a former college professor. The men of the 20th Maine were asked to hold Little Round Top at all costs because, if they didn't, the attacking Confederate forces would be able to outflank and destroy the Union divisions holding the rest of the line. Chamberlain's men held valiantly until they ran out of ammunition. Chamberlain used a technique he had learned in studying Greek warfare. He had his men fix bayonets and swung his companies of men like a giant door against the oncoming rebel forces. They chased the Confederates down the hill and held until relief arrived. During the war, Colonel Chamberlain was wounded six times in combat and awarded the Congressional Medal of Honor for his heroism.

# SCRIPT SUMMARY: THE DEFENSE OF LITTLE ROUND TOP

The Defense of Little Round Top describes one of the most important battles of the Civil War. The narrator sets the time and place: July 2, 1863, on the heights of a small hill called Little Round Top during the pivotal battle of Gettysburg. Colonel Joshua Lawrence Chamberlain and his small regiment of men have been asked to defend the hill at the extreme end of the Union lines against a tough, battle-hardened unit of Southern soldiers. They are outnumbered and running out of ammunition.

The two soldiers, a corporal, and a sergeant discuss the desperate situation they face against the Rebel soldiers who have been attacking them. They also express their reservations about their commander, Colonel Chamberlain, who was a college professor before the war. They admire his courage and leadership but are afraid he will be outmaneuvered by the veteran war commanders of the South.

Colonel Chamberlain explains the situation to them and describes a maneuver he wants the men to make based on a famous Greek battle of long ago. He has his men swing into battle like a revolving door and charge down the hill with bayonets fixed to their rifles because they are out of ammunition. The attack is successful and his men defeat the attacking Southern forces. The next day, Lee's forces are defeated in the larger battle of Gettysburg.

## Assignment

Read the readers' theater script about the assault of Little Round Top at the Battle of Gettysburg. Work within your group to prepare for the performance. Share your interpretation of the script.

## Extensions: Writing and Literature

- Write your own readers' theater script based on one of the events listed below or another one related to the Civil War period. After practicing your script, share your performance with the rest of the class.

  A slave decides to run away from his owner and fight for the North.

  General Lee surrenders to Grant at Appomattux.

  Abraham Lincoln and his cabinet debate the Emancipation Proclamation.

  A group of soldiers prepare for battle at Shiloh, Antietam, or any other battle.

- Read *Sarny* by Gary Paulsen. Choose an episode or chapter in this Civil War novel as a subject for a readers' theater script. Perform the script for the class.

# SCRIPT: THE DEFENSE OF LITTLE ROUND TOP

This script is an account of the assault on Little Round Top, a critical hilltop during the second day of the Battle of Gettysburg and its defense by a beleaguered regiment, the 20th Maine Volunteers, and their extraordinary commander, Colonel Joshua Lawrence Chamberlain. There are six speaking parts.

**Narrator:** The time is late afternoon of July 2, 1863, at the climactic Battle of Gettysburg. A small, beleaguered, and outnumbered regiment of about 320 Northern soldiers—the 20th Maine volunteers—is holding the crucial heights on Little Round Top, a hill overlooking part of the battlefield. They are at the very end of the Union lines. If the attacking Alabama forces can outflank them or push them off the hill, then the entire Union army is at risk of being overrun and destroyed by the armies of General Robert E. Lee. The commander of the 20th Maine volunteers, Colonel Joshua Lawrence Chamberlain, is a former professor of philosophy, foreign languages, and history from tiny Bowdoin College in Maine.

**First Soldier:** Boys, we're in a fix. It looks like half the Rebel army out there is getting ready to charge up this hill. I don't see how we can hold out.

**Second Soldier:** They're coming up on the weak side to our left, too. This is going to be a rough one, boys.

**First Soldier:** I don't know what to think of our colonel, either. He is not a regular officer, you know. He was a college professor before the war.

**Corporal:** Well, he's done fine so far. After all, none of us were soldiers before the war.

**First Soldier:** But he taught literature and poetry and philosophy. What does he know about war? These Southern officers will outsmart him for sure.

**Sergeant:** They're getting ready to charge. Our biggest problem is that we are short of ammunition, and nobody can get any to us. We're totally cut off.

**Narrator:** Colonel Chamberlain joins his soldiers to explain the situation and his plan.

**Colonel Chamberlain:** Men, listen well. The enemy intends to turn our flank. If we lose the left flank, they will take this hill and command the heights for their final assault on Gettysburg tomorrow. Every soldier knows it is essential to hold the high ground.

**Second Soldier:** They have got us pretty badly outnumbered, Colonel. Maybe more than two to one. On top of that, we're just about out of ammunition, and we have no artillery support. How are we going to hold them off?

**Colonel Chamberlain:** We are going to use a military tactic I learned while teaching Greek history. It was used in a Greek war thousands of years ago. Be prepared to move forward at my command. Hurry, men, we have no time to lose. The enemy is advancing.

**First Soldier:** I hope the colonel knows what he is doing. If he does not, we're going to end up as Confederate mincemeat.

**Sergeant:** Form up, men! We've no time to waste. Ready! Here they come!

**Colonel Chamberlain:** Stand firm, ye boys of Maine, for not once in a century are men permitted to bear such responsibilities for freedom and justice, for God and humanity, as are placed upon you.

**Corporal:** Ready! Aim! Fire!

Reload! Fire!

Reload! Fire!

Fire at will!

**Second Soldier:** We are out of bullets. We have used up everything we have! What will we do, Colonel?

**Sergeant:** We are trapped in the open. We've got only two choices—advance or retreat—and we have no bullets left!

**Colonel Chamberlain:** If we retreat here, the Union could lose the war. Retreat is out of the question.

Gentlemen, fix bayonets!

**Corporal:** Fix bayonets! Charge!

Charge bayonets! Attack! Attack!

**Narrator:** The men of the 20th Maine charged down the hill against their attackers. Their bayonet charge eventually swept the Confederate forces back, and survivors of the 20th Maine regiment held Little Round Top. The Union army did win at Gettysburg. Colonel Chamberlain was seriously wounded in six separate battles and twice reported dead on the field of battle. However, he survived to accept the surrender of one Confederate army at the end of the war. He returned home to teach at Bowdoin College, where at one time or another he taught every subject except math. He also became the governor of Maine.

# READER'S RESPONSE: THE DEFENSE OF LITTLE ROUND TOP

## Directions

- These discussion activities and questions may be used in small groups or with the entire class. They may also be used by the actors as a part of their preparation for the reading.

- Refer to the script "The Defense of Little Round Top" when responding to all questions. You may also find useful facts in the background section and in other readings about the Civil War.

- Make notes on the lines provided below each question before your group discussion.

## General Discussion

1. What were the military challenges faced by the 320 soldiers of the 20th Maine?

_____

_____

_____

2. Why did the men of the 20th Maine have to hold the heights at Little Round Top?

_____

_____

3. How do the soldiers of the 20th Maine feel about the ability and leadership of their colonel?

_____

_____

_____

4. How important was the defense of Little Round Top to the Northern army at Gettysburg?

_____

_____

_____

## Making It Personal

The battles of the Civil War, including Gettysburg, were extremely costly in terms of lives lost and soldiers seriously wounded and disabled. Why do you think so many men on both sides of the war fought so hard for so many years?

_____

_____

_____

_____

How do you think you would have responded if you had lived in Civil War times? What events or arguments would have affected your decision?

_____

_____

_____

_____

# READERS' THEATER

# HUGH GLASS AIN'T DEAD YET

# BACKGROUND: HUGH GLASS AIN'T DEAD YET

## Mountain Men

A fashion fad among wealthy men in Europe and America in the early 1800s led to the origin of the mountain men. Hats made from the thick fur of beavers became popular. Fur companies were organized to hunt for beaver. They hired adventurous, independent, and courageous men of many backgrounds to go to the far streams of the American west and into the heart of Indian tribal lands to trap beavers.

Some mountain men had been French fur trappers. Others were from various Native American tribes, such as the Delaware and the Iroquois. Others were African-Americans. Many mountain men were the restless sons of pioneers and immigrants. Mountain men paid for their own weapons and supplies that were expensive. They dressed in buckskin like many Native Americans. They usually lived on their own in the wild and met once a year at a rendezvous where they traded their furs for gold and supplies. Some fur trappers worked in a group like those in the script on the following pages. Beaver trapping began in the early 1800s and died out around 1840 as a major business.

## Hugh Glass

Hugh Glass may have been the toughest mountain man of all. He fought a grizzly bear with a Bowie knife and was torn to pieces and knocked unconscious. Two trappers, Jim Bridger and John Fitzgerald, had agreed to stay with him until he died. They became frightened by the possibility of hostile Indians and took Hugh's belongings, leaving Hugh to die alone. Glass eventually woke up and crawled to a river for water. Eating scraps from a buffalo killed by wolves, other dead animals, and roots, he began a 200-mile journey walking and crawling across the plains to Fort Kiowa. Glass then hunted down the trappers who had abandoned him. He never found Fitzgerald who simply vanished from the West. He found Jim Bridger but did not harm him.

## Jim Bridger

Jim Bridger was a very young and inexperienced trapper when he left Hugh Glass to die. He went on to become the best known of the mountain men. He was respected by many people that he guided through the West, including army units and wagon trains. Bridger couldn't read, but he could draw a detailed map of every area he ever explored. He traveled widely through the Rocky Mountains, and he was the first white trapper to discover the Great Salt Lake.

# SCRIPT SUMMARY: HUGH GLASS AIN'T DEAD YET

"Hugh Glass Ain't Dead Yet" is based on one of the most incredible survival stories in American history. The narrator sets the scene for the audience. Hugh Glass, a fur trapper in Major Henry's trapping expedition, gets into a fight with a grizzly bear. He kills the bear with his knife but is near death himself. Major Henry doesn't want to endanger his men by waiting in hostile Indian country for Hugh to die. He asks for volunteers to wait with Glass through the night, when he is expected to die, and bury him in the morning.

Jim Bridger, an inexperienced trapper called a *greenhorn*, offers to stay with Hugh. The other trappers are afraid Bridger will get killed by Indians or lead them to Henry's new camp. Another trapper, John Fitzgerald, agrees to stay with Bridger. The two men wait through the night, but Fitzgerald becomes increasingly worried and insists that they leave Hugh to die. The men take his rifle and other possessions (his "possibles" bag), and catch up to their friends.

Glass recovers consciousness and realizes he's been abandoned by the two men who were supposed to care for him. He starts crawling at night on his hands and knees toward a fort over 100 miles away. He crawls over very rough terrain and is nourished only by dead and decayed animals he finds. He keeps himself alive by planning what he is going to do to the two men who were supposed to stay with him. Weeks later, he crawls into Fort Kiowa and slowly recovers his strength.

Hugh borrows a gun and supplies and sets out to find Jim Bridger. He nearly scares Bridger to death when they meet, but he takes the young man's inexperience into account and lets him live.

## Assignment

Read "Hugh Glass Ain't Dead Yet." Work with your group to prepare for the performance and share your interpretation of the script with the class.

## Extensions: Writing and Literature

- Write a script based on one of the events listed below or another one related to the westward movement.

  John Colter's miraculous escape from the Blackfoot Indians

  A young boy goes beaver trapping with a mountain man.

  Life on the trail with the Donner Party

  Life in a Plains Indian community

- Read *Little House on the Prairie* by Laura Ingalls Wilder or *Mr. Tucket* by Gary Paulsen. Write a script based on a chapter or episode in one of the books. Share your performance with the rest of the class.

# SCRIPT: HUGH GLASS AIN'T DEAD YET

There are six speaking parts in this script about mountain man Hugh Glass.

**Narrator:** Mountain man Hugh Glass was hunting alone when he was cornered by a grizzly bear. He shot the bear with his single-shot rifle, but it just enraged the beast more. Hugh fought the grizzly with his knife, but he was no match for the large bear and its razor-sharp claws. Other trappers found the dead bear lying on top of Hugh who was clawed to ribbons, drenched in blood, and barely alive. One of the trappers sewed up Hugh's wounds. Major Henry and the other trappers waited through the night expecting Hugh to die, but he was still alive in the morning.

**Major Henry:** Men, the Indians are on the warpath. I can't risk everyone here just to bury old Hugh, good a man as he is. Hugh must be part wildcat himself to have killed that old grizzly bear. Still, it's clear to me he'll not last the day, and we've got to move on. I'd like a volunteer to stay with old Hugh, bury him proper, and then catch up with us.

**Jim Bridger:** I'll stay. I always liked Hugh. He's taught me a lot. I'll bury him deep and catch up with you.

**Trapper:** Major, you can't leave that young'un alone here with Hugh. He's too green and has no experience in these mountains. The Injuns'll kill him for sure here or follow him to us.

**Major Henry:** That's true enough. I need a volunteer to stay with Bridger and do right by Hugh.

**Narrator:** The major's request for a volunteer was met with silence as the men glanced first at each other and then the ground. They knew the danger of being alone in a country with a tough tribe of Plains Indians on the warpath. There were no takers.

**Major Henry:** Well, I understand the danger, but it's only fair to Hugh. I'll tell you what. I'll give 40 bucks to the man who stays with our young greenhorn here and helps him bury Hugh.

**John Fitzgerald:** I guess I'll do it. That's a good piece of change, and from the look of that old cuss he ain't gonna last long anyhow.

**Major Henry:** Mount up, men. We'd best be moving out. You two take care and do right by old Hugh. Fitzgerald, you see that young Jim here keeps his scalp.

**Narrator:** Major Henry and the rest of the trappers left. Jim Bridger busied himself trying to make Hugh comfortable. Fitzgerald started pacing about the camp and checking the area for signs of Indians. The two are still there at nightfall. Hugh Glass was still alive, but each raspy breath he took seemed like it was the last one he would ever draw.

**John Fitzgerald:** What's the matter with that old man? He ought to be dead by now. It's nigh onto dark, and I can feel trouble. We should've been done and gone by now.

**Jim Bridger:** Hugh's still breathing. We said we'd stay till he passed on.

**John Fitzgerald:** He's the same as dead. That old man's never gonna move from where he's lying. I tell you, we need to leave whilst we can.

**Jim Bridger:** He'll be dead by morning. We can do our duty by him and then move on.

**Narrator:** But Hugh wasn't dead by morning. He was still barely breathing, but Fitzgerald could not stand it anymore.

**John Fitzgerald:** We need to go. We're fools to stay here. The man is dead as a corpse. He just doesn't know it yet.

**Jim Bridger:** I reckon you're right, but what will we do with old Hugh?

**John Fitzgerald:** You take his rifle and skinning knife. I'll take his possibles bag. He's got some good traps and stuff. Make him comfortable, and let's go. Time's a'wasting. We'll tell the others Hugh died, and we buried him. Nobody'll be the wiser.

**Narrator:** They caught up with the others in a few days and reported Hugh's death, but Hugh Glass didn't die. He lay a few days in his half-conscious state and then woke up one evening to find himself coated in blood, starving, and parched with thirst.

**Hugh Glass:** The Major left young Bridger and Fitzgerald to bury me. I heard him. Where did those two rascals go? Where's my rifle? My knife's missing, too, and my possibles bag is gone. They done took everything and skedaddled. Figured I was dead, they did. Well, I'll show them. Old Hugh ain't dead!

**Narrator:** Unable to walk or even stand up, Hugh crawled down to a stream, drank all he could, and started crawling southeast in the direction of Fort Kiowa. He found a dead bison that had been mostly eaten by wolves. He ate some of the rotten carcass, took some of the bones to gnaw out the marrow, and crawled on.

**Hugh Glass:** Be lucky to make a mile tonight. I'll chew out the bone tomorrow. I'll sleep during the day. It ain't but two hundred miles to Fort Kiowa. I'll make it if the wolves or the buzzards don't get me. And those two buzzards that left me to die, you just wait 'till I catch your hides.

**Narrator:** Hugh Glass slept through the day and crawled at night. He ate anything dead he could find and licked water from the underside of leaves and small pools of water that he found along the way. Weeks later he crawled into Fort Kiowa. Hugh spent months there recovering his strength and remembering his promise to himself about the men who left him. Hugh left Fort Kiowa with a borrowed rifle and supplies, following a rumor that Jim Bridger was trapping on his own on the Northern Plains. He sneaked up on Bridger's camp months later while Jim was cooking dinner.

**Hugh Glass:** Freeze, you yellow-bellied coward! I got you now!

**Jim Bridger:** Who? What do you want? Who are you?

**Hugh:** Scared you, didn't I? Don't you recognize Old Hugh?

**Jim:** You can't be! Hugh Glass is dead! You must be a spirit!

**Hugh Glass:** I ain't dead yet. No thanks to you! Left me to die, you did. Yellow-dog coward!

**Jim:** But you were near dead. That old grizzly bear had clawed you up something fierce! You was bleeding from a dozen cuts, but you just kept breathing. I'm sorry, Hugh. I deserve to die, I guess. Go ahead and get it done.

**Hugh Glass:** I ain't gonna to kill you—much as you deserve it. I'm taking your age into account. Young folks tend to do stupid things right often. You'll learn if you get any older.

**Narrator:** Hugh Glass never caught up to John Fitzgerald. He just disappeared and was never seen again. Jim Bridger, however, went on to become one of the most famous mountain men—a man who was highly respected for his courage and for keeping his word.

# READER'S RESPONSE: HUGH GLASS AIN'T DEAD YET

## Directions

- These discussion activities and questions may be used in small groups or with the entire class. They may also be used by the actors as a part of their preparation for the reading.
- Refer to the script "Hugh Glass Ain't Dead Yet" when responding to all questions. You may also find useful facts in the background section.
- Make notes on the lines provided below each question before your group discussion.

## General Discussion

1. How did Hugh Glass survive after he was abandoned by Bridger and Fitzgerald? What did he do to save himself?

_____

_____

_____

_____

2. Why did Jim Bridger and John Fitzgerald leave Hugh Glass and did they have good reasons to leave?

_____

_____

_____

_____

3. Why do you think Hugh Glass was able to endure so many terrible dangers and threats to his life from thirst, starvation, and wounds and still survive?

_____

_____

_____

_____

## Making It Personal

What would you have done if you were left with Hugh Glass and didn't expect him to live? What choices would you have and which one would you be likely to choose?

_____

_____

_____

_____

Could you have done what Hugh Glass did to survive? Which of the things he did would have been the hardest to do or to endure? Give your reasons.

_____

_____

_____

_____

# READERS' THEATER

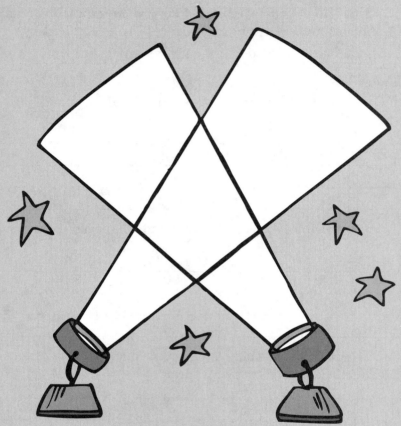

# FIRST FLIGHT

## BACKGROUND: FIRST FLIGHT

### Brothers on a Mission

Wilbur and Orville Wright were brothers and bicycle mechanics who became fascinated by the idea of flight. They designed and built kites and later gliders and soon focused their energies on building a heavier-than-air machine that would fly on its own power. They took their gliders to Kitty Hawk, South Carolina, where they did more than a thousand trials. In 1902 and 1903, they used their experience with gliders to design and build the *Flyer*, a plane with an engine and propellers that they designed and built. They tried to patent their new ideas, but the U.S. Patent Office wasn't interested.

Other amateur air enthusiasts were getting close to success in making and flying a true airplane. In particular, Samuel Langley of the Smithsonian Institution had several near successes. The brothers took their *Flyer* to some sand dunes called Kill Devil Hills near Kitty Hawk in December 1903. They built a 60-foot monorail to help guide the *Flyer* as it was launched. On December 14, Wilbur made an unsuccessful attempt to get the *Flyer* into the air.

On December 17, Orville took the controls and launched into a 27 mile an hour wind. Three men from a lifesaving squad and two other local men helped set up the monorail. They also became witnesses to history as Orville Wright made the first flight, lasting 12 seconds and traveling 120 feet. A second flight with Wilbur at the controls lasted 15 seconds and traveled 175 feet. The third trial was 15 seconds long and traveled 200 feet. The last flight lasted 59 seconds and went 852 feet. Before they had an opportunity to make a fifth flight, a heavy gust of wind caught the *Flyer* and blew it across the dunes, wrecking the plane completely.

*Orville and Wilbur Wright*

Even though the brothers notified the press and had photographs to prove their accomplishment, little notice was taken of their achievement at the time. It was almost five years before they were generally acknowledged as the first to fly. In that time, the Wright brothers and other daring young men in flying machines made extraordinary progress in building and flying planes.

# SCRIPT SUMMARY: FIRST FLIGHT

"First Flight" is a dramatic reenactment of the first four successful flights by the Wright brothers on December 17, 1903. The script describes the preparations for the flight and the arrival of three lifesaving crew members and two other interested young men from neighboring towns. The brothers had tried their newly designed plane three days before without success. They had great hopes for the plane because they had designed and made a new motor and propellers for their *Flyer*. They were also anxious to achieve success before some other person made the first successful flight.

The men help the brothers get the plane on the monorail and cheer as Orville Wright manages to hold the plane aloft for 12 seconds. Each successive flight goes a longer distance with the fourth flight lasting 59 seconds and traveling 852 feet. It was a great accomplishment, and the brothers had both photographic proof and eyewitnesses. The brothers sent a telegram to their family who did notify the newspapers. However, the press did not seem very interested. It would be five years before people generally acknowledged the Wright brothers as making the first flight.

## Assignment

Read the script entitled "First Flight" about the dramatic early flights of the Wright brothers. Work within your group to prepare for the performance. Share your interpretations of the script.

## Extensions: Writing and Literature

- Write and perform your own readers' theater script based on one of the events listed below or another one related to the early days of aviation.

  Imagine the pilot's fears and feelings as he is making his first flight. Write a script in which the pilot expresses his emotions out loud.

  Write a script describing your feelings if you got to fly an airplane.

- Read *The Wright Brothers: How They Invented the Airplane* by Russell Freedman or another account of their pioneer work in aviation. Choose a chapter, episode, or event in the story to use as the basis for a readers' theater script. Write and produce the script for your class.

# SCRIPT: FIRST FLIGHT

This script is an account of the first flights made by Wilbur and Orville Wright on December 17, 1903. There are eight speaking parts.

**Narrator:** On December 17, 1903, two determined brothers who had spent the last seven years trying to fly are ready to launch the *Flyer*, their latest and most advanced aircraft. Orville and Wilbur Wright had started with kites and graduated to gliders, constantly improving their designs. They designed and built a motor and propellers for their aircraft. They shipped the plane in pieces from their home in Dayton, Ohio, to Kill Devil Hills on the Outer Banks of North Carolina, near the small village of Kitty Hawk where they had flown their gliders in previous winters. Three members of a lifesaver corps have come to help as well as W.C. and Johnny from neighboring towns.

**Wilbur:** Men, thank you for coming. I'm glad you saw our red flag asking for help.

**Willie:** We're glad to see you boys. Adam and Daniels and I are bored anyway. You liven up the place. There haven't been any lives for us surfmen to save lately.

**Johnny:** I'm from Nags Head and heard of you fellows. I'd love to see that machine get into the air.

**W.C.:** I heard about you boys. I want to see this contraption fly.

**Narrator:** The brothers flipped a coin and Orville won. He would be the pilot.

**Orville:** I hope we make it today. Samuel Langley's plane almost flew over the Potomac River last week. If we want to be first, it's got to be now.

**Wilbur:** You're right. Somebody's going to fly first. It ought to be us.

**Adam:** What can we do?

**Wilbur:**      Boys, help us lay out the track of this monorail on which the *Flyer* will be sliding along until it becomes airborne.

**Daniels:**      I'll take the picture.  Someone has to prove this machine flew, and I think today is the day.

**Narrator:**      While the men set up the monorail, Orville and Wilbur shook hands for several moments.

**Orville:**      I guess it's time.  I think this one will fly.

**Wilbur:**      Take care, brother.  I think you're right.

**Daniels:**      I think those boys know this is the one.  I can feel it in my bones.

**Adam:**      Me, too.

**Wilbur:**      She's starting.  Run along the sides, boys, and steady the wings.

**Narrator:**      The plane wobbled and shook and climbed into the sky.  It sailed and bumped and jostled through the air and then landed on a ridge of sand 120 feet away after a 12-second flight.  The men raced to congratulate Orville.

**W.C.:**      You flew!  You actually flew!

**Orville:**      We did it!  It's the first time in the history of the world in which a machine carrying a man raised itself by its own power into the air in full flight.

**Adam:**      Great job, Orville.  I'm going to brag forever about what I saw today.

**Daniels:**      You did it, boys.  Great job!

**Wilbur:**      Guys, let's set it up and fly again.  It is my turn this time.

**Narrator:**      The men hauled the plane back to the monorail and set it up again.

**Johnny:** He's off.

**Adam:** Go, Wilbur! Ride like the wind!

**Daniels:** It flew 15 seconds this time.

**Adam:** The *Flyer* traveled 175 feet this time.

**Narrator:** They set up for a third flight with Orville back at the controls.

**Johnny:** This time it went 200 feet in 15 seconds. That's the best yet!

**Narrator:** At noon, Wilbur made the fourth flight.

**Daniels:** That's the record! You were in the air 59 seconds!

**Willie:** You flew 852 feet! What a flight! Boys, we'll never forget this day.

**Narrator:** A sudden wind gust came up across the dunes and whipped the *Flyer* as they were getting ready for a fifth flight hoping this time to fly the four miles to the village of Kitty Hawk. The men raced to save the *Flyer,* but the machine was broken beyond repair.

**Orville:** Let's walk to Kitty Hawk, Wilbur. I've got a telegram to send to Dad in Dayton.

**Narrator:** The telegram read: SUCCESS FOUR FLIGHTS THURSDAY MORNING ALL AGAINST TWENTY-ONE-MILE WIND STARTED FROM LEVEL WITH ENGINE POWER ALONE AVERAGE SPEED THROUGH AIR THIRTY ONE MILES, LONGEST 59 SECONDS INFORM PRESS HOME FOR CHRISTMAS.

Newspapers were informed, but little notice was taken of the Wright brothers' achievement even though they had photographs to prove what they did. It would be almost five years before it was generally recognized that the Wright Brothers had been the first to fly successfully in a heavier-than-air machine.

# READER'S RESPONSE: FIRST FLIGHT

## Directions

- These discussion activities and questions may be used in small groups or with the entire class. They may also be used by the actors as a part of their preparation for the reading.
- Refer to the script "First Flight" when responding to all questions. You may also find useful facts in the background section.
- Make notes on the lines provided below each question before your group discussion.

## General Discussion

1. Why do you think men came to help the Wright brothers with the *Flyer*?

_____

_____

_____

2. How do the Wright brothers demonstrate their persistence and courage? Give examples.

_____

_____

_____

3. Why do you think the brothers picked a beach for their flights?

_____

_____

_____

4. What is the importance of the Wright brothers' first flight?

_____

_____

_____

## Making It Personal

Would you have been willing to ride flat on your belly on the center wing of the plane as the brothers did on their *Flyer*? Give your reasons.

_____

_____

_____

What inventions or discoveries are being worked on today that may be as important as the first flight by the Wright brothers? Explain your answer.

_____

_____

_____

# READERS' THEATER

# TRIANGLE TERROR

# BACKGROUND: TRIANGLE TERROR

## Industrial Revolution

The Industrial Revolution is one of the most important events in human history. It has changed human life in every part of the world, made and destroyed the fortunes of nations, and dramatically altered the planet itself. This revolution began in England in the mid-1700s and quickly spread to the United States and Europe. In the course of the last 200 years, it has spread throughout the world. This revolution was spurred by new inventions that made products more cheaply, by the development of large amounts of capital (money available to investors and factory owners), and especially by cheap labor.

## Mistreating Workers

The deliberate actions of the owners in paying very low wages and the availability of large numbers of people desperate for work led to conditions in factories which were incredibly cruel, extremely dangerous, and brutally competitive. Men and women worked long hours without adequate breaks for food and personal needs. Factory owners constantly looked for ways to make workers do more work for less pay. No provisions were made for proper sanitation, protection against accidents and fires, adequate ventilation for breathing, or safety in operating machines.

## Triangle Shirtwaist Factory Fire

The Triangle Shirtwaist Factory in New York was typical of many manufacturing businesses. The owners hired many poor, immigrant women who had no place to get better work. The factory owners fired any workers who tried to form unions or organize complaints against the company. The mill girls who worked in this clothing factory were locked into the building. They suffered from tuberculosis and other diseases that affected the lungs. They had almost no break time except a few minutes to eat a midday meal. The stairways were locked during working hours. Their pay was barely enough to live on and not nearly enough to support a family.

Almost all factories had the same rules, and many had experienced fires and serious accidents that killed or crippled workers. The fire that started in the Triangle Factory spread at extraordinary speed through the building. Workers were unable to get into the locked stairwells, and many girls were forced to choose between being burned alive and jumping out the windows to the pavement below. The fire occurred on March 25, 1911, and killed 146 of 500 workers. The incident aroused the nation and eventually led to rules allowing unions to organize and laws related to safety and personal rights being enforced in factories in the United States.

# SCRIPT SUMMARY: TRIANGLE TERROR

"Triangle Terror" is a dramatic account of the intersecting lives of three girls working in the Triangle Shirtwaist Factory in March of 1911. The narrator introduces Nell, an Irish immigrant, Clara, an immigrant from Russia, and Hannah, a Jewish girl from Poland. All of the girls recognize that the job they have is better than starving or doing piecework, a system that paid even less money to those desperate for work. They discuss their fears and angers frankly. The girls hate being locked into the factory. They lose pay for being even a minute late, they are humiliated by frequent inspections by supervisors to make sure they are not stealing cloth, and they know conditions in the plant are very unhealthy and dangerous.

Fire erupts in a pile of cloth, and the mill girls rush to save a girl who is being engulfed in flames. Suddenly, they realize the entire floor is on fire. They can't get out the exits or down the stairs because they are locked. The girls try to help their friends and look for a way out. Realizing that their only choice is to break the windows and jump from the 8th floor, they hold onto each other and jump. The three friends die in the fall as did 146 workers during the fire. The narrator explains that this accident warned the nation of the dangers of factory work, but it would take another 25 years before Congress passed the first laws governing worker safety in factories.

## Assignment

Read the readers' theater script "Triangle Terror." Prepare for the performances and share your interpretations of the scripts with the class.

## Extensions: Writing and Literature

- Write a script based on one of the events listed below or another one related to the Industrial Revolution.

    The struggles of a group of steelworkers, miners, or factory workers who try to start a union

    A group of factory workers are forced to take a pay cut.

    Immigrants new to the country discuss their problems at a factory.

    The reactions of people who see the catastrophe as the girls jump out of the Triangle Shirtwaist Factory

- Read *Ashes of Roses* by Mary Jane Auch about the Triangle Shirtwaist Factory fire. Write a script based on an episode or chapter in the book. After practicing your script, share your performance with the rest of the class.

# SCRIPT: TRIANGLE TERROR

This script tells about mill girls who worked at the Triangle Shirtwaist Factory in New York City, where a fire in March 1911 killed 146 workers. There are four speakers.

**Narrator:** In the early twentieth century, many young girls were employed in textile mills. Nell is newly arrived from Ireland, Clara is a Russian immigrant, and Hannah is a Jewish immigrant from Poland. All are mill girls working at the Triangle Shirtwaist Factory in New York City in 1911.

**Nell:** I hate those locked doors on each floor. I feel like I'm trapped in a prison. What do they think we're going to do—run away? We are eight floors up. There is no place to go.

**Clara:** They're so afraid we'll sneak in two minutes late. What's the difference? They dock our pay anyway for any lost time, even if we're sick or hurt.

**Hannah:** They lock the doors to make sure we don't just walk out some day in one angry group. They fear our strength.

**Nell:** I hate the noise, too. The loud, screeching sound of all these machines can drive you insane. It makes my head hurt.

**Clara:** This factory reminds me of Russia with the police and soldiers constantly checking your papers and insulting you.

**Nell:** The women bosses here are always inspecting our clothes when we leave to make sure we don't steal a few inches of ribbon or a scrap of cloth. They treat us like common thieves.

**Hannah:** It's humiliating. We'd be a lot better off if we could get every working girl here to join the union and fight for our rights together.

**Nell:** It won't work. There are thousands of other girls who'd be happy to have our jobs. We don't make much money here, but we're not starving or doing piecework sewing just to survive.

**Hannah:** We're slaves here—factory slaves. We don't have any power to get better pay, work fewer hours, or to stay home when we're sick. Look at poor Agnes over there. She's had that cough for weeks, and it's getting worse. She got it from all of the dust and lint in the air here.

**Clara:** The windows aren't even open to provide ventilation. Agnes can't stay home or see a doctor, because they'd fire her for missing work. She's the sole support of her crippled mother, but she could die from tuberculosis or some other disease. She's getting thinner and weaker every day.

**Nell:** Lots of the girls have hacking coughs, but we've no choice. They fired Elizabeth when she lost three fingers in the machine she worked on. Since she couldn't work, she was no use to them anymore. What can we do?

**Clara:** I smell something burning. Somebody's machine must be overheating.

**Hannah:** Look, there's smoke!

**Nell:** That's a lot of smoke. That's no damaged machine. I think it's coming from the pile of waste fabric. Oh Lord, look at the blaze! The building is on fire!

**Clara:** Lenora's on fire! Help me smother the flames!

**Narrator:** The girls rush to gather cloth and smother the flames on Lenora's dress, and they see that piles of cloth are spurting flame. The roar of the fire drowns out the sound of the other machines, and dozens of girls are suddenly screaming and running toward the doors. The building is in pandemonium.

**Nell:** The doors are locked! Find a foreman! Get a key!

**Clara:** Smash the door! We have to get out! We'll be burned alive!

**Hannah:** The doors won't break! Check the others!

**Narrator:** Girls pile together to push the doors in desperation and die crushed or suffocated by smoke. The three friends can see flames spreading over the entire floor. Machines and cloth, walls and ceilings are all are on fire. The thick smoke is choking and blinding them. Girls are collapsing. Many are now on fire.

**Hannah:** The doors are blocked. We can't get out that way. We've no choice but to jump through the windows.

**Nell:** We'll be cut to pieces, and it's eight floors to the ground. We'll die for sure!

**Hannah:** Probably, but anything's better than fire. Help me smash this window. Agnes and Harriet just jumped.

**Clara:** I'm burning! Help me!

**Hannah:** Nell, grab Clara! Hang on now, girls! Jump!

**Narrator:** The firemen's nets on the street broke, and the girls fell to their deaths. Of the 500 workers in the factory, 146 died either from the fire or from jumping out windows. The Triangle Shirtwaist Fire on March 25, 1911, was a tragedy that awakened the nation to the dangers of factory life. It would be more than 25 years, however, before tough, stringent laws would be passed to prevent future catastrophes like this one.

# READER'S RESPONSE: TRIANGLE TERROR

## Directions

- These discussion activities and questions may be used in small groups or with the entire class. They may also be used by the actors as a part of their preparation for the reading.

- Refer to the script "Triangle Terror" when responding to all questions. You may also find useful facts in the background section.

- Make notes on the lines provided below each question before your group discussion.

## General Discussion

1. Why did conditions in the factory remind Clara of conditions in Russia?

   _____

   _____

2. What rules and regulations made work in the Triangle Shirtwaist Factory dangerous and unpleasant?

   _____

   _____

3. Do you think there are places in the world today where workers are treated as badly as they were in this factory? Explain your answer.

   _____

   _____

4. How do you think American workers got rules changed to prevent these terrible accidents from happening today? How did they succeed?

   _____

   _____

5. What disadvantages did the girls have that made it easier for the factory owners to be unconcerned about the workers' health and safety? List several reasons the girls could be taken advantage of.

   _____

   _____

## Making It Personal

Would you have worked in the factory if it was your only chance for a job in 1911? Explain your reasons.

   _____

   _____

Would you have jumped out of the window as the girls did in the story because there was no other way out? Describe your feelings.

   _____

   _____

# READERS' THEATER

# CHILD'S WORK

## The Dark Side of the Revolution

The Industrial Revolution led to a massive increase in the production of goods and services for consumers and greatly reduced the cost of producing those goods and services. The dark side of the revolution was the relentless drive by factory owners to increase their profits at the expense of their workers. Employees worked 12 to 14 hours a day, six days a week without sick days, vacations, or time off to take care of family needs. Workers who couldn't keep up their workload lost their jobs. No welfare system and no health care program existed to help workers. Factory owners hired young women as mill girls because they could pay them less. They hired newly arrived immigrants who could be taken advantage of, and they soon found that child labor made their profits even greater.

## Child Labor

There were no rules against employing children in factories. Boys and girls under ten years old were routinely used in textile mills in very dangerous jobs. Because they were small and agile, some children were used to run under machines and tie loose threads. Seven-year-old boys worked as "doffers" replacing the bobbins of thread in textile factories. Girls of the same age worked as spinners, brushing lint from machines and tying broken threads. Many children developed spinal deformities, limps, scars, and other physical injuries from their work.

Immigrant children worked along with their parents in canneries shucking oysters, cutting beans, peeling apples and tomatoes, and processing other foods. Ten-year-old boys were sitting above rivers of coal separating slate and stone from the coal flowing by. Many fell into the moving coal and were mangled or killed. All had coughs produced by the coal dust. At the age of twelve, they became coal miners.

These children had no schooling. They worked 12 to 14 hours a day just like adults. School was not mandatory, and families with working children desperately needed the money children earned just to eat. Children earned less than half of what adult men were paid.

# SCRIPT SUMMARY: CHILD'S WORK

"Child's Work" is a script formatted like a "You Are There" documentary. The narrator sets the time period (1911) and introduces Jennifer, the host. Jennifer interviews three children who work in a mine, a factory, or a cannery.

Dennis is the first child she interviews. He is a coal breaker in a West Virginia mine. He describes his job that is literally to sit above a slowly moving river of coal and pick out pieces of rock and chunks of materials that are not coal. Like most of the boys hired to do this job, he lied about his age and started work at the age of 10, four years before the legal age of 14. Dennis describes how friends were crushed to death and that he has lost two fingers on the job.

Next, Jennifer interviews Molly, a spinner in a Georgia textile mill. She is an eight-year-old girl whose job is to brush lint off the machines and tie broken threads on the bobbins for 12 hours every day. Her younger brother is a "doffer" who replaces spools of thread. They are both paid pennies a day.

The third child laborer is six-year-old Jacob who cracks oysters and cuts out the meat. He works with his parents and has been doing this work since he was four. He makes 10 to 15 cents on a good day.

None of the children has ever been to school nor will they ever have a chance to learn to read and write. Many children will die or be seriously hurt by diseases, accidents, and lack of proper food.

## Assignment

Read the readers' theater script "Child's Work." Prepare for the performances and share your interpretations of the scripts with the class.

## Extensions: Writing and Literature

- Write a script based on one of the events listed below or another one related to child labor.

    One day in the life of a child working in a coal mine or a factory

    One day in the life of an entire family working in a cannery or mill

    Imagine that you and your family are immigrants to the United States working in a factory, cannery, or on a farm. Tell your story.

- Read *Esperanza Rising* by Pam Munoz Ryan. Use one episode or a chapter as the basis for a readers' theater script about life for a migrant farm worker family.

- Read *Lyddie* by Katherine Paterson. Use one chapter or episode as the basis for a script about a mill girl's life in the 1840s.

# SCRIPT: CHILD'S WORK

In this script three children who worked at different jobs in 1911 are interviewed. There are five speakers.

**Narrator:** Welcome to the Living History Channel and our continuing series "A Look at America's Past" hosted by Jennifer Sloan. Each week she takes us back in time to a moment in American history that gives us a glimpse of life during that period.

**Jennifer:** Good evening, everyone. Tonight we will travel back to 1911, rewind the reels of history, and meet a group of children. These children are hard at work in our nation's mills, canneries, factories, mines, and farms. Our first guest is Dennis McKee, a young coal breaker in a West Virginia mine. Dennis, how long have you been working at this coal company?

**Dennis:** Well, Ma'am, I been working here about two years now.

**Jennifer:** How old are you?

**Dennis:** I'm 12, but I told'em I was 14 because the law says you gotta be 14. The foreman knew but don't really care anyhow. Most of us boys start work here when we're about 10. If inspectors come around, they just hide us for a couple hours, but then they also dock our pay. That don't seem fair though.

**Jennifer:** What do you do at the mine, Dennis?

**Dennis:** I'm a coal breaker. I sit in a little box with coal moving under me and pull out pieces of rock and other stuff that ain't coal. You got to be real careful though. Two of my friends got caught last month and was carried down the chute and died. I lost two fingers myself a while back.

**Jennifer:** Our next guest is Molly Jackson who works at a Georgia textile mill as a spinner. How old are you, Molly, and what is your job?

**Molly:** I'm almost nine. I been working here every day since I was about seven—'cept on Sundays, of course. Me'n the other girls start work directly at six in the morning. We work 12-hour shifts. You can't be even a minute late or they docks your pay an hour. We spinners go up and down the aisles between the spinning machines and brush the lint off the machines.

**Jennifer:** Is it always this dusty in the mill?

**Molly:** All this dust in the air is mostly just tiny bits of cloth. We can't let it get on the machines, or they'll clog up and break down. The thread on the bobbins sometimes breaks, so we also have to tie the broken ends together so the machines don't stop. Girls are better at that cause our fingers is smaller and faster. There ain't no time to rest.

Boys are mostly doffers. They replace the spools of thread on the machines. That's tricky work. My younger brother caught his foot in a machine and busted it up bad. He's still working though.

**Jennifer:** Have you ever been to school, Molly?

**Molly:** I'd like to go to school, but it ain't likely. Nobody in my family can read or do sums. We all work once we can walk. Even though I only earn a few cents a day, we needs the money to eat and pay the rent on the shack that's our home.

**Jennifer:** Have you ever been to the doctor for your cough?

**Molly:** Everybody in the mill has a cough. All us spinners gets one after being here a while. Some kids die from it, but most of us is luckier. Can't afford no doctor.

**Jennifer:** Our third guest is Jacob Caldwell. He is an oyster shucker in a Mississippi cannery. Jacob, how old are you and what kind of work do you do?

**Jacob:** I'm six now, but I been workin' with my parents since I was four. It took a while to learn how to crack open them oysters and shuck out the meat. I was pretty quick to learn how to use the shuckin' knife, but if you ain't extra careful, you'll slice off a finger or two like my brother did.

**Jennifer:** Your hands are scarred and bleeding. Wouldn't you rather be in school?

**Jacob:** Can't afford to go to school. We need the money to eat. They pay five cents for a pail of shucked oysters, and I make about 10 or 15 cents on a good day. The shells are sharp and cut your hands, but they scar over and harden. Shrimp are worse to shuck cause the acid eats the skin off your fingers and makes holes in your clothes and boots. I don't specially like startin' work at three in the morning, either.

**Jennifer:** Well, that wraps up our show for today. I want to thank my three guests for joining us and telling us about their lives.

**Narrator:** Today, you have met three young children who worked in the United States in 1911. They were among tens of thousands of children who had to work to help their families survive. They could not go to school, had very little time for play, and many died early from disease, accidents, and lack of proper food. It was a national tragedy. Thank you for joining us on "A Look at America's Past."

# READER'S RESPONSE: CHILD'S WORK

## Directions

- These discussion activities and questions may be used in small groups or with the entire class. They may also be used by the actors as a part of their preparation for the reading.

- Refer to the script "Child's Work" when responding to all questions. You may also find useful facts in the background section.

- Make notes on the lines provided below each question before your group discussion.

## General Discussion

1. Why do you think the coal mine owners hire children like Dennis instead of adults? Look for several reasons.

   _____
   _____
   _____

2. Which child—Molly, Jacob, or Dennis—is the most mistreated by the owners of the businesses where they work? Give your reasons for your choice.

   _____
   _____
   _____

3. Why do you think children in this country are not allowed to work in factories, mines, and canneries today? How do you think the laws got changed?

   _____
   _____
   _____

4. Do you know of countries in the world today where child labor is allowed? What could be done to eliminate child labor in other countries?

   _____
   _____
   _____

## Making It Personal

Which job would you least want to do if you were a child working in 1911? Explain your choice.

   _____
   _____
   _____

How do you think each the three children might have felt if they had been allowed to go to school instead of work every day? What would their attitude at school be?

   _____
   _____
   _____

# READERS' THEATER

# WEST TO HOPE

# BACKGROUND: WEST TO HOPE

## The Dust Bowl: Drought and Black Blizzards

The people living on the Great Plains in Southern Kansas, the panhandle of Western Oklahoma, and Northern Texas were especially hard hit during the Great Depression. This area became known as the Dust Bowl. Farmers had plowed under the tough prairie grasses that had fed the native buffalo of the plains and planted wheat that didn't hold the soil well. The Great Plains was hit by a long and brutal drought between 1931 and 1937. There was virtually no rain, but clouds of grasshoppers swept across thousands of acres eating everything in their path. The dust bowl years featured horrific dust storms called *black blizzards* with the dust blowing at gale speeds.

The endlessly blowing dust forced people to cover their faces with wet cloths to help them breathe. The wind stripped away the topsoil making the land on the plains much less fertile and likely to nurture crops when rain did come. The inability to grow crops caused many farmers to lose their farms to banks that held loans based on the buildings and land. More than two million people were forced to leave their farms and travel someplace else to live. Families loaded what few possessions they still owned on a horse-drawn wagon or an old jalopy. Many families had nothing but handcarts or children's wagons.

## California Dreams

Over one million people headed for California where they hoped to find farm jobs. Those with cars drove until they ran out of gas and then waited with a few feet of garden hose until a kindly stranger drove by and let them siphon a few gallons of gas out of their own gas tanks. Some people walked all the way or got occasional help from strangers as they headed west.

Families lived on lard sandwiches, boiled cabbage, corn bread, coffee grounds, carrot tops, apple cores, and garbage they could scrounge from farms or town dumps. The water supply, usually streams or ditches, became polluted because it was used for drinking, washing clothes, bathing, and toileting. Contagious diseases and lice were widespread. Many children and older people died from malnutrition, illness, and injuries. These migrants were not wanted anywhere, and many communities just forced these homeless families to move on. They had no place to go and no hope for work. When they arrived in California, they seldom found any work there, either.

# SCRIPT SUMMARY: WEST TO HOPE

The script "West to Hope" describes the pain, suffering, and failures of one family uprooted from their farm and forced to travel west looking desperately for work and food. The narrator introduces the Goodman family from the Oklahoma panhandle who lost their farm to the bank when they could not make their payments. The dust and wind destroyed their crops and land. They took what little they had on a broken-down old jalopy and headed west hoping to find work on farms in California.

Along the back roads of Oklahoma and along Route 66 across the Southwest, the family watched their old vehicle fall apart. They begged for gas from strangers and pushed the car when they had to. The children foraged for a few potatoes or vegetables left in the fields, and for birds, rabbits, and anything else which might be eaten.

The Goodman's meet other families at a campground and hear the discouraging news that California may have no work available either. Nonetheless, they are determined to press on. They have nothing to go back to and very little hope of a better future where they are going. They keep pushing ahead in a river of misery hoping for a rainbow or a miracle.

## Assignment

Read the readers' theater script "West to Hope." Prepare for the performances and share your interpretations of the script with the class.

## Extensions: Writing and Literature

- Write a script based on one of the events listed below or another one related to life during the dust bowl.

  Life on a dust bowl farm

  A family on the road during the depression

  A father loses his job during the depression and cannot find another.

  A school closes during the depression because the town has no money to fund it.

  Children go to school one morning and find a homeless family camped there.

- Read *Out of the Dust* by Karen Hesse. Use one episode or a chapter as the basis for a readers' theater script about life for a dust bowl family.

- Read *Treasures in the Dust* by Tracey Porter. Use one episode or a chapter as the basis for a readers' theater script about life for children during the dust bowl years.

# SCRIPT: WEST TO HOPE

This script tells about life during the dust bowl.  There are seven speakers.

**Narrator:** Black blizzards of dust have pounded the Oklahoma panhandle for five years.  The Goodman family watched the crops on their prairie farm dry up and die because of the lack of rain.  Their cattle and chickens ate weeds and smothered in the dust.  Mr. Goodman lost his land to the bank when he could not make the payments on his mortgage.  The family loaded their few remaining possessions on an old, broken-down jalopy with boards on the back to hold their suitcases and the children.

**Dad:** I hate to leave this farm, but we have no choice.  I can't get work anywhere.  Everybody here is as bad off as we are or worse.  They say there's work in California.  We just have to give it a try.  We've got enough gas to get us to Route 66, I think.

**Annie:** How are we going to get there, Dad?  We don't even have money for gas.  Our food won't last us but a few days.

**Mom:** We'll hope in the Lord, Annie.  You take care of your brothers James and Woody, and make sure they don't fall off.

**Narrator:** The family traveled along the dust-swept roads of western Oklahoma and into eastern New Mexico where they turned onto Route 66, the long road leading to California.  Dad took out a piece of hose a few feet long.

**Dad:** We're out of gas and lucky we got this far.  We'll push our jalopy along this level stretch and hope for a kind motorist to pass along.

**Woody:** Why does Dad grab that old hose every time someone passes?

**Annie:** He's hoping for a good Samaritan.  Maybe this car will have one.

**Dad:** Mister, I could sure use a few gallons of gas if you can spare it.

**Traveler:** I haven't much myself, but you can siphon out a couple of gallons with that hose. You folks look to be in worse trouble than I am.

**Annie:** Night's coming on, Dad. What will we do?

**Dad:** You kids can sleep by the side of this road. Your Ma and I will share the cab. You kids check that field. There may be some roots left from the harvest. Maybe some stunted ears of corn got missed. Check anyways. Anything near the road's gonna be long gone. Lots of folks like us have come before.

**Narrator:** The family continued along Route 66, traveling a few miles a day. Soon they faced even greater trouble.

**Dad:** The left rear tire is shot. There's no tread left on the tire. I can't patch the tube any more. I've wrapped the tire with cloth, but you children will have to walk from now on. Ma, we've got to dump some of the things in the back just like we've seen other families do.

**Mom:** I hate to leave those two kitchen chairs. They're the only furniture we have left.

**Dad:** It can't be helped. You kids keep a sharp eye out for food. There might be rabbits or other critters we could snare. Look for birds, too. Woody, keep some stones in hand to chuck at anything you see. We're out of flour, and all that's left are two ears of corn. Look sharp.

**James:**  Annie, I miss home. I even miss school.

**Annie:**  Me, too.  We hardly went this year because we couldn't afford the clothes and the supplies.  I hated it when some of the girls laughed at my feed-bag dress and burlap jacket, but we're going to be way behind if we ever go back to school.

**Narrator:**  The family continued its long trek westward going through New Mexico and Arizona, finally entering California.  They were pushing their jalopy now with the kids taking turns steering.

**Dad:**  There's a camp ahead with people and what looks like a ditch with water.  We'll stop there and get the news.  Maybe someone will have some food.  There sure is a lot of coughing.

**Narrator:**  They pitched camp and joined other families just as poor, starved, weak, and exhausted as they were.  They used the water in the ditch to clean up, but it was already badly contaminated with the dirt and filth of those who had already been there.  The news they heard was not good. Nobody had found steady work.  Most of the children and older people were sick with typhoid, dysentery, and other diseases.

**Dad:**  The news isn't good, but we aren't quitting.  We're going to keep on traveling until I find a job or we run into the Pacific Ocean.  Our only hope is out west.  People from the county gave me a few gallons of gas, so we'd keep moving.  They don't want us here, either.

**Annie:**  I sometimes wonder if the whole world isn't broke and on the move. All we've seen is a river of misery.  Well, maybe there's a rainbow somewhere.  We'll keep looking for one.

# READER'S RESPONSE: WEST TO HOPE

## Directions

- These discussion activities and questions may be used in small groups or with the entire class. They may also be used by the actors as a part of their preparation for the reading.
- Refer to the script "West to Hope" when responding to all questions. You may also find useful facts in the background section.
- Make notes on the lines provided below each question before your group discussion.

## General Discussion

1. Why did the Goodman family have to leave their home?

_____

_____

_____

2. Which person was most important in keeping the family alive on the road to California? Explain your choice.

_____

_____

_____

3. What personal dangers could the Goodman family have encountered on the their trip?

_____

_____

_____

## Making It Personal

Put yourself in the place of the Goodman family. What would you have done to save your family?

_____

_____

_____

How would you have felt about going to school if you were in Annie's place and had only feed-bag clothes? What would your attitude at school be?

_____

_____

_____

Annie, James, and Woody helped their parents on the trip to California. What could you have done to help your family if you were starving and pushing a car like the Goodman family?

_____

_____

_____

Do you think Annie will find her rainbow? What do you think will happen?

_____

_____

_____

# READERS' THEATER

# HOOVERVILLE BLUES

# BACKGROUND: HOOVERVILLE BLUES

## The Great Depression

Millions of people lost their homes in the U.S. during the Great Depression (1929–mid 1930s). Many people who had owned homes lost their jobs and could no longer make the payments to the bank on their loans and their homes were sold at auction. Others lost their jobs and couldn't afford rent for even the cheapest or most rundown house or apartment. Families moved in with relatives when they could, but many families had no one to help them.

## Hoovervilles

Many homeless families lived in shacks made from cardboard, discarded wood, and scrap metal. They sometimes lived in the rusted-out shells of abandoned automobiles. Many of these shacks were built at the edges of towns and cities, often near a town dump where people could search for food, clothing, and trash that had been discarded. They called these neighborhoods "Hoovervilles," a reference to President Herbert Hoover. These people thought Hoover had not done enough to help ordinary people deal with the their lost homes and jobs.

## Life in a Hooverville

Food was cheap if you had the money, but many people were so poor that starvation and malnutrition were common. Mothers often made soups with whatever they might have. Some days a soup bone, cabbage, carrot tops, and a few spoiled potatoes would feed several families. Although farmers were dumping milk, burning some crops, and killing hogs and cattle because prices were so low, children were regularly going to bed hungry.

Clothes were cheap but not if you did not have any money. Mothers used every scrap of cloth to make children's clothes. Many used animal feed sacks and burlap bags to make dresses, trousers, and shirts. Many children went barefoot, even in the winter. Others shoved cardboard into the soles of worn-out shoes. Newspapers, called "Hoover blankets," were often used to keep warm at night, especially by the very poor, like those living in Hoovervilles.

Children often did not get to attend school because they were too embarrassed to go to school clothed in rags or sacks. Many communities would not allow children in the Hoovervilles to attend their schools.

# SCRIPT SUMMARY: HOOVERVILLE BLUES

The script "Hooverville Blues" describes the life of the Rankin family in their new home, a rusted-out old car in a junkyard. They have insulated it with cardboard boxes and stray boards hoping to cut out the wind, if not the cold. Their daughter Claire has found a few chunks of coal along the railroad tracks to burn for heat. The railroad police ran her off before she could collect more. Janey found stones to cook on. They meet other neighbors in this Hooverville and share some scraps of food and junk to make a fire.

The children cannot go to school because the city officials won't let them, but they discover that another resident of the shantytown is a former teacher who lost her job during this depression. She is trying to teach reading and arithmetic without books, papers, or pencils. The oldest children find some discarded newspapers which they will use as "Hoover blankets" to insulate the children from the cold night wind. The family has no solution to the contaminated water and lack of sanitation or toilet facilities at the camp. Despite all of their problems, they still hope for brighter days, an end to the depression, and the destruction of this Hooverville.

## Assignment

Read the readers' theater script "Hooverville Blues." Prepare for the performances and share your interpretations of the scripts with the class.

## Extensions: Writing and Literature

- Write a script based on one of the events listed below or another one related to depression-era life.

    A family has to leave its home because the father lost his job.

    A family tries to live in a Hooverville.

    A father loses his job during the depression and cannot find another.

    Children go to school dressed in feed sacks and burlap bags because that is all they have to wear.

- Read *Bud, Not Buddy* by Christopher Paul Curtis. Use one episode or a chapter as the basis for a readers' theater script about life during the depression.

- *Soup for President* and *A Day No Pigs Would Die* by Robert Newton Peck are other books that deal with depression life and could be used as source books for your scripts.

# SCRIPT: HOOVERVILLE BLUES

This script tells the story of a family whose lives have been changed by the Great Depression. There are eight speakers, but some readers could do two parts.

**Narrator:** The Rankin family has a new home. When Mr. Rankin lost his job making cloth in a factory, he could not pay the rent on their small apartment. Mr. Rankin was unable to find any other job. He tried shining shoes and selling apples, but every street corner in the city had someone already doing that. It's 1933, and the Depression has been going on for almost four years. The only place the Rankins could find to live was the Hooverville on the edge of their city. Mr. and Mrs. Rankin and their six children have scrounged together some cardboard trash and a few wooden boxes,

**Dad:** Well, Millie, we were lucky to find this old rusted-out car. It must have been sitting here for ten years.

**Mom:** I cleaned what I could, John, but the rust is just everywhere. We'll put those pieces of cardboard the kids found on the seats, so the children won't be poked with the rusty springs sticking out through the seats. At least it will stop the wind and snow. God knows, nothing will cut the cold of these winter nights.

**Jerry:** Mom, we found these old pieces of wood by the railroad tracks. We can brace them up against the car and weave the cardboard in between the wood.

**Claire:** Dad, I found some coal left along the tracks from the railroad engines. We couldn't take any more because the railroad police ran us off.

**Mom:** We can use it for cooking and a little warmth this evening. Janey found some flat stones and bricks that we can heat up to keep our feet warm tonight.

**Janey:** I'm hungry. Isn't there anything to eat?

**Mom:** I know, child. We all are. We'll have to make do with what we have.

**Narrator:** As the family begins to build a fire, a neighboring couple come from their cardboard box shack a few feet away.

**Neighbor:** Folks, we see that you're new here. We've been here five months now. You have some coal. We've got some cardboard scraps and trash from the dump to burn. We've a little food to share. The potatoes are soft and the apples are partly rotten, but we've some to share if you're of a mind to.

**Mom:** We'd be grateful for the food and the company, neighbor. We have a few coffee grounds, part of a cabbage that's pretty wilted, and some carrot tops my oldest son found in someone's garden.

**Claire:** Do any of the kids here go to school?

**Neighbor:** No, the city fathers don't even want to admit we're here. We're an embarrassment. The cops have run us out several times, but folks just drift back and start over. After all, people have to get rid of their trash somewhere. We're just trash ourselves to some people.

**Claire:** I miss school. I miss my friends, the teacher, and my lessons.

**Neighbor:** Well, there's not much you can do about your friends or teacher, but young Ruthie Johnson on the other side of this Hooverville shantytown has a bunch of kids she reads with and teaches some figures to. They've got no paper or books, but she uses the dirt to teach letters and figuring. She'll help any child. Ruthie was a teacher who lost her job in this depression. Her husband was killed trying to jump a freight train.

**Narrator:**   The oldest two Rankin boys show up with their arms full of newspapers and join the group, reaching hungrily for the soup their mother has made.

**Richard:**   Mom, we found piles of these newspapers that people had thrown away in an alley. Most are clean and can be used to make Hoover blankets. We can burn the others.

**Mom:**   Thank you, boys. These should help keep you kids a bit warmer tonight.

**Neighbor:**   Have all the kids sleep tight together at night and surround them with those Hoover blankets. They'll hold in their body warmth and keep the cold out.

**Mom:**   I can't keep the children clean or clothed. I never thought I'd see the day I dressed my children in trash from the dump and feed bags from the store.

**Neighbor:**   The worst problem is water. That ditch along the edge of camp is totally filthy. Have your kids drink snow for water when they can. At least it's clean.

**Dad:**   Neighbor, do you think this depression will ever end? I'm afraid I'm going to lose my whole family. My two youngest kids are too skinny for words, pale as snow and always coughing.

**Neighbor:**   I hope so. I'd like to see everybody get jobs and homes, and then I'd be glad to come burn this Hooverville to the ground.

**Dad:**   The day that happens, I'll be here to lend you a hand.

# READER'S RESPONSE: HOOVERVILLE BLUES

## Directions
- These discussion activities and questions may be used in small groups or with the entire class. They may also be used by the actors as a part of their preparation for the reading.
- Refer to the script "Hooverville Blues" when responding to all questions. You may also find useful facts in the background section.
- Make notes on the lines provided below each question before your group discussion.

## General Discussion
1. Why is the Rankin family living in a rusted-out old car in a Hooverville?

   _____

   _____

2. Why don't the Rankin children go to school?

   _____

   _____

3. Do you think people could face the problems caused by a future depression with large numbers of people out of work, homeless families, and starving children? Explain your answer.

   _____

   _____

   _____

4. Why do you think newspapers were called Hoover blankets and the shantytown was called Hooverville?

   _____

   _____

5. Do you think anybody lives like the Rankins today in America or other countries? Explain.

   _____

   _____

## Making It Personal
How would you feel if you were not allowed to go to school because nobody wanted to admit you were a part of their town or city?

_____

_____

Suppose you and your entire family lost your home and your parents lost their jobs and had no income to feed or clothe you. What would you do? How would you feel?

_____

_____

_____

# READERS' THEATER

# ON OMAHA BEACH

# BACKGROUND: ON OMAHA BEACH

## World War II

World War II was the most catastrophic war in the history of the world. It killed more people, destroyed more property, and uprooted the lives of more people than any previous war. At least 17 million soldiers and more than 35 million civilians were killed. Millions of soldiers and civilians were wounded and missing.

World War II officially began on September 1, 1939, when Germany invaded Poland, and the governments of France and England honored their treaty obligations and went to war in defense of Poland. In April 1940, German troops easily invaded Denmark and Norway. In May 1940, Germany invaded and conquered Belgium, the Netherlands, and most of France. In April 1941, German troops invaded Greece and Yugoslavia. In June of 1941, Hitler's armies invaded the Soviet Union.

After the attack on Pearl Harbor on December 7, 1941, the United States joined England and Russia in the war to defeat Germany and Japan. For nearly three years, the allied powers battled Germany and Japan in a long series of fiercely fought battles. The enormous industrial capacity of the United States supplied the planes, ships, and weapons used to slow the German war machine.

## D-Day at Normandy

The reconquest of Europe began with the invasion of Normandy on the coast of France. On June 6, 1944, the Allies launched the greatest amphibious assault in history at Normandy. Omaha Beach was one of several code designations for sectors of the beach. More than 5,000 ships and 175,000 men participated in this invasion. The fighting was extremely fierce and often hand to hand along the system of trenches, pillboxes, and machine gun positions protecting the coast from the Allied troops. By nightfall of the first day, the Allies had secured some positions at enormous cost in lives. They gradually pushed back the German lines. The Allied forces finally broke through stiff German resistance in late July 1944 and rolled eastward liberating Paris in August and pushing on toward Germany.

# SCRIPT SUMMARY: ON OMAHA BEACH

The narrator sets the time and place for this script—the landing on Omaha Beach at Normandy, France, by a platoon of soldiers, six of whom have speaking parts in addition to the narrator. The lieutenant leads them off the boat, and Private Scott is immediately shot in the chest.

As they get through the water to the beach, the Lieutenant is shot, and the sergeant leads them across the beach to a partially sheltered ridge at the base of the hill. The Corporal and C.J. set explosives to destroy a concrete pillbox filled with enemy guns. The men throw grenades and attack the enemy bunker. The script ends with the destruction of this enemy position, but many more heavily fortified areas remain. The narrator explains that despite the terrible cost, the Allied troops have begun the liberation of Europe from the Nazis.

## Assignment

Read the readers' theater script "On Omaha Beach." Prepare for the performances and share your interpretations of the scripts with the class.

## Extensions: Writing and Literature

- Write a script based on one of the events listed below or another one related to World War II.

    A refugee escaping the terrors of war

    A World War II battle scene such as Iwo Jima, the tank battles in Northern Africa, or the Battle of the Bulge

    A scene for the home front during the war

    Life in a Japanese relocation camp

    Life in a Nazi concentration camp

- Read *Number the Stars* by Lois Lowry. Use one episode or a chapter as the basis for a readers' theater script about life in an occupied country during World War II.

- Read *The Journal of Scott Pendleton Collins: A World War II Soldier* by Walter Dean Myers. Use one episode or a chapter of this fictional diary as the basis for a readers' theater script about a soldier's life during World War II. After practicing your script, share your performance with the rest of the class.

# SCRIPT: ON OMAHA BEACH

Omaha Beach was the Allied code name for one of the main landing points during the Normandy landings on June 6, 1944. There are seven speaking parts in this script.

**Narrator:** This morning, June 6, 1944, the greatest amphibious assault in modern warfare is occurring on the beaches of Normandy along the coast of occupied France. A fleet of 5,000 ships and 175,000 troops from the United States, Great Britain, Canada, and France are beginning the liberation of Europe from the Nazi oppressors who have conquered and controlled most of the continent. As the scene begins, a squad of four American soldiers is waiting anxiously in a small landing craft moving slowly toward Omaha Beach.

**Lieutenant:** Men, we're 30 seconds from dropping the gangplank. Remember your training. If you wade too slowly through the water, you're going to be perfect targets for the German gunners on the hills overlooking the beach.

**Private Scott:** I'm scared.

**Corporal:** It's nothing to be ashamed of, Scott. We're all scared.

**Sergeant:** I tell you Private, I've been through a lot of battles from the Kasserine Pass in Northern Africa to Sicily and up through Italy. They were terrible, but this is the worst I've ever seen. There are a lot of men dying out there.

**Lieutenant:** Go! Go! Go! Get to the beach!

**Sergeant:** Move out!